SHOWDOWN

# SHOWDOWN

## CONFRONTING MODERN AMERICA IN THE WESTERN FILM

### JOHN H. LENIHAN

UNIVERSITY OF ILLINOIS PRESS
URBANA, CHICAGO, LONDON

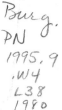
© 1980 by the Board of Trustees
of the University of Illinois
Manufactured in the United States of America

Library of Congress Cataloging in Publication Data

Lenihan, John H.     1941–
Showdown, confronting modern America in the western film.

Bibliography: p.
Includes index.
1. Western films—History and criticism.
2. National characteristics, American.   I. Title.
PN1995.9.W4L38   1979      791.43′0909′32      79-25271
ISBN 0-252-00769-7

*To Mom and Dad*

# CONTENTS

ILLUSTRATIONS

*Stills from Selected Films*

ACKNOWLEDGMENTS

Without the encourage-
ment and perceptive guidance of David Grimsted, writing about
Westerns for a history Ph.D. at the University of Maryland might
have remained an audacious fancy. He was particularly attentive
and adept in helping me articulate coherently what often seemed
a hopeless tangle of ideas about the more than five-hundred films
I had studied.

Frequent intellectual jousts with James Gilbert forced me to
rethink initial interpretations. Walter Rundell, Jr., Wayne Cole,
and Myron Loundesbury were helpful in matters of style and
clarity, while Ray Smock offered useful suggestions to strengthen
the dissertation for publication. Special thanks to Stuart Kauf-
man for his unwavering support and good counsel throughout
this project.

Patrick Sheehan and Joe Balian made available the marvelous
film collection and viewing facilities of the Motion Picture Section of the Library of Congress. Anne Schlosser, librarian at the
American Film Institute (Charles K. Feldman Library) in Beverly Hills went out of her way to point me in the direction of
manuscript holdings in the Los Angeles area. She and the li-
brarians at USC, UCLA, and the Motion Picture Academy of
Arts and Sciences granted full access to their special collections.

There is no substitute for interviewing filmmakers to understand what goes into the fashioning of a motion picture. During
the summer of 1973, Delmer Daves, Gordon Douglas, Joseph
Kane, George Marshall, Winston Miller, Aaron Rosenberg,
James Webb, and Richard and Elizabeth Wilson invited me to

their homes or offices to share with them their past experiences in writing, producing, and directing Westerns.

From the University of Illinois Press, I received the expert assistance of Frank Williams, Harriet Stockanes, and especially my copyeditor, Rita Zelewsky. May the final product amply repay their professional attention.

Ginger Vallery Lenihan performed the unenviable chore of styling polished drafts from my almost illegible scribble. But my regard for her, as for my son Erik, cannot be fully measured in terms of this study.

More than anyone else, my parents Gladys and Howard Lenihan made possible whatever I have achieved thus far, including this book. Only they can appreciate the degree to which *Showdown* was inspired by the many evenings the three of us spent at the Admiral and Granada theaters. And Dad, you were right all along: "There's nothing like a good Western."

# SHOWDOWN

CHAPTER ONE

# INTRODUCTION

I N THE SEARCH FOR NEW AP-
proaches toward understanding popular thought, historians have
only begun to tap the vast resources of popular culture distributed
by America's publishing houses and communications media. In
this study I have chosen to analyze the content of one important
cultural formula, the western motion picture, in order to demonstrate its relation to major political, intellectual, and social issues
and trends since World War II and, in turn, to suggest some of
the assumptions, concerns, and attitudes of the society that has
rendered this genre so popular.

Scholars representing a variety of intellectual perspectives,
including the historical, have long recognized the importance of
movies in American society.[1] Lewis Jacobs in 1939 based his
reputable history of the American film on the premise that films
"reflect . . . the changing temper of the times."[2] While Jacobs
and others have demonstrated in very general terms that films
mirror shifting moods and issues of a particular period, academic
historians have commonly settled for acknowledging the importance of movies as a national pastime without paying adequate attention to their content or implications with regard to
the broader climate of social thought. Historians traditionally
have been inclined to analyze great thinkers and artists seriously,

[1] A lengthy bibliography in I. C. Jarvie, *Movies and Society* (New York:
Basic Books, 1970), lists many historical, sociological, psychological, and aesthetic analyses of the American films.
[2] Lewis Jacobs, *The Rise of the American Film* (New York: Teachers
College Press, 1939), p. 283.

while dismissing radio, television, the movies, and popular fiction as escapist entertainment for the masses.[3]

Since its inception the motion picture industry has by commercial necessity adapted its product to variations in public mood to attract the largest possible audience. As Paul Mayersburg stated in his brief examination of the Hollywood film industry, "Just because Hollywood films are made for a mass audience, they do unconsciously reveal mass preoccupations, what we think about ourselves and the world."[4] With the decline in movie attendance after World War II, producers' sensitivity to public tastes and sensibilities assumed even greater urgency.

The study of a single genre is especially revealing of how a particular form is modified in accordance with the constantly changing concerns and attitudes of a society. No genre has retained more continuous popularity than has the Western; nor is any genre more involved with fundamental American beliefs about individualism and social progress. Many American and European film scholars have approached the Western as a peculiarly American cultural form. In the words of one prominent student of the popular arts, "Surely no twentieth century American needs to have the Western's importance as a cultural form demonstrated to him. Uncountable Westerns mark the course of American history."[5]

[3] With respect to histories of the post-1945 period, it is encouraging to see recent attempts to address the content of movies and other popular arts. See, for example: William L. O'Neill, *Coming Apart: An Informal History of America in the 1960s* (Chicago: Quadrangle Books, 1971); Douglas T. Miller and Marion Nowak, *The Fifties: The Way We Really Were* (Garden City, New York: Doubleday, 1977). Professional historians Robert Sklar and Thomas Cripps have recently contributed scholarly film histories, a field hereafter left to journalists and other academicians; see Robert Sklar, *Movie-Made America: A Social History of American Movies* (New York: Random House, 1975); Thomas Cripps, *Slow Fade to Black: The Negro in American Film, 1900–1942* (London: Oxford University Press, 1977). Susan S. Tampke and William H. Cohn edited a section of *Journal of Popular Culture* XI:I (Summer 1977), in which historians suggest what their profession can contribute to the study of popular culture. The possibilities of historical inquiry are also explored in Paul Smith, ed., *The Historian and Film* (Cambridge: Cambridge University Press, 1976).

[4] Paul Mayersburg, *Hollywood: The Haunted House* (London: Penguin Books, 1967), p. 71.

[5] John Cawelti, *The Six-Gun Mystique* (Bowling Green, O.: Bowling Green University Popular Press, 1971), p. 1.

Only recently has the Western been thoughtfully examined as the product of a particular social and cultural climate. George N. Fenin and William K. Everson's *The Western: From Silents to the Seventies* (1973) and John Tuska's *The Filming of the West* (1976)—to date the most comprehensive histories of the western movie—mention, without fully developing, the formula's contemporary aspects. The Western since World War II has been the principal subject of Philip French's *Westerns* (1974), Jennie Caulder's *There Must Be a Lone Ranger* (1975), and Will Wright's *Six Guns and Society* (1975). While providing useful insights into the Western's contemporary character, these works remain limited in their selection of films and elaboration of relevant postwar issues and ideas. The relationship between films and the society they address is far more obvious and extensive than has been suggested to date.

The post–World War II years offer a number of attractions for studying the Western. This was a period of acute national self-examination of America's direction in foreign affairs, the social assimilation of ethnic minorities, and the ability of the corporate welfare state to serve the collective needs of a mass society while respecting individual rights and interests. Conspicuously rich from an intellectual standpoint, the postwar decades include numerous political and social observations about the national character, as well as the nation's values and institutions, as America faced new and greater problems at home and abroad. *Organization man, lonely crowd, alienated individual, conformity, concensus, anxiety,* and *complacency* are among the terms employed by social analysts to suggest liabilities of the fifties' affluent society.[6] In the 1960s this questioning assumed even greater proportions, with the Vietnam War, ghetto and campus unrest, and the emergence of a New Left and counterculture to challenge traditional beliefs and institutions. These variations in critical sensibility found expression not only in

[6] The titles of many prominent sociological and historical evaluations of the post–World War II era reflect these characteristics: David Riesman et al., *The Lonely Crowd* (New Haven, Conn.: Yale University Press, 1950); William H. Whyte, Jr., *The Organization Man* (Garden City, N.Y.: Doubleday Anchor Books, 1956); Carl Degler, *Affluence and Anxiety* (Glenview, Ill.: Scott, Foresman, 1975).

political and intellectual circles but in mass entertainment, including the western motion picture.

Another attractive characteristic of this period is the availability of so many films. The Library of Congress and television, each offering a disproportionate number of post-1945 productions, are the principal sources for the more than five hundred Westerns viewed for this study. These range from most major ("prestige") attractions to such staple western films as those starring Randolph Scott or Audie Murphy. Plot summaries from pressbooks and film reviews were consulted for those Westerns that could not be seen. Excluded are the serials and most B series films (Gene Autry et al.), because too few were readily available to constitute an adequate sample and because, in any case, they were dying out by the early fifties.

Throughout much of the postwar period, the Western was the most significant of film formulas in terms of popularity and innovation. John Cawelti estimated that in 1958 no less than fifty-four feature Westerns graced America's screens, slackening in succeeding years only to enjoy revival in 1967 under impetus of the Italian imports of Sergio Leone.[7] Although the Western proved resilient amid a general decline in movie business during the fifties, sixties, and early seventies, since 1976 the genre has become nearly extinct, even though movies in general have survived.

Since 1945, filmmakers have more fully realized the ideological richness and thematic possibilities of the western formula. Because television western series duplicated and usurped the B western motif, Hollywood compensated with more lavish productions but also with more imaginative and complex western fare than television could afford on a weekly basis. Notions of heroism and villainy were rendered ambiguous, with greater emphasis given to psychological dimensions and social problems. Screenwriters and directors more obviously adapted the western format to modern topics and concerns. This self-consciousness has produced mixed results in terms of quality, but it has insured

[7] John Cawelti, *Six-Gun Mystique*, p. 2. He also notes that in 1958 Westerns constituted 10.64 percent of the year's published fiction, while a year later eight of the top ten Nielsen-rated television shows were Westerns.

a clearer incorporation into the Western of contemporary concerns and, occasionally, of a more poignantly complex handling of themes related to the western myth.

The following chapters demonstrate the Western's relevance to changing contemporary issues and outlooks in America since World War II. A thematic analysis at the most obvious narrative level will clearly illustrate implications pertinent to commonly recognized topics of historical interest: the Cold War, racial equality, and the problem—characteristic of intellectual writings —of individual identity and freedom in an increasingly regulated but uncertain mass society. No claim is made to have exhausted the various meanings that a film may have for its makers or audience. But the topical characteristics explored here are sufficiently overt to show that Westerns did in fact communicate matters of great political and intellectual importance.

More important than any single Western is the totality of Westerns that reflect significant formula variations. *The Gunfighter* (1950) had negligible popularity, but its handling of individual alienation and social weakness characterized many subsequent Westerns of the decade. The significance of an individual film, in terms of either artistic merit or popularity, matters less than the recurrent pattern of themes and ideas in other Westerns. Popular films are naturally more important in determining acceptable filming ideas and assumptions, but here also the single film must be set against the larger body of Westerns. *Shane* (1953) and *How the West Was Won* (1962) drew large audiences, yet the same brand of classic optimism was much less evident in most other Westerns—popular or not—of the period. Only by treating Westerns collectively can what was unusual and passing be distinguished from what was common and pervasive.

Will Wright's recent sociological analysis of Westerns in *Six Guns and Society* (1975) illustrates the danger of determining social significance from a small selection of films based solely on popularity. Wright's limited film selection allowed him to delineate clear thematic patterns; but these patterns are questionable in that he has failed to recognize the pervasiveness of themes and ideas not accounted for by his list of top moneymakers. After finding only three socially critical, or what he labels "transition,"

Westerns (*Broken Arrow* [1950], *High Noon* [1952], *Johnny Guitar* [1954]) that meet his qualifications as popular films during the fifties, Wright wonders why the transition theme was so short-lived: "If it was truly an important stage in the development of the Western myth, should there not be more instances of it? I cannot say precisely why there were not more films with this structure."[8] The fact is that there were many other Westerns of the fifties that exhibited his transition theme, either totally or in part, however short of Wright's arbitrary box office standard they may have fallen.

The influence of individual filmmakers on the meaning and implication of a film will be acknowledged whenever there is sufficient evidence, but the focus will be primarily on the film itself. The question of individual vision is especially difficult given the collective corporate nature of film production. The producer, director, writer, star, and studio policy influence the final product in varying degrees. Press interviews of film personalities, such as *Playboy*'s encounters with John Wayne and Sam Peckinpah, are helpful in their sketches of strongly assertive minds whose marks are clearly imprinted on their films. Taped and transcribed interviews of producers, directors, stars, and writers (some conducted by the author) have been consulted but were used sparingly and with considerable caution; the films not only speak for themselves but often turn out quite differently from the specific intentions or policies governing their production. Any importance attached to individuals who influence a particular film must be weighed against the fact that a motion picture is a composite creation of many types of artists, technicians, and businessmen. This is not to dispute the *auteur* theory of attributing the style and meaning of a film to its director, or to deny qualitative differences that distinguish art from mediocrity, but rather to suggest social meanings that transcend any one filmmaker. John Ford or Howard Hawks contributed a dis-

8 Will Wright, *Six Guns and Society: A Structural Study of the Western* (Berkeley: University of California Press, 1975), p. 85. By placing Westerns such as *Stagecoach, Apache,* and *One-Eyed Jacks* outside the transition category, Wright tends to underestimate the extent of a socially critical vision even among the box-office winners he chooses to emphasize.

tinctive point of view and style but also addressed problems and issues that are reflected in other Westerns as well as in the larger society and culture.

The question of measuring a film's influence or impact on a society continues to elude verification. Walt Disney's Davy Crockett adventures obviously affected the sale of coonskin caps, as other Westerns influenced the sale of cap pistols and cowboy outfits. The same cause and effect relationship has not yet been applied convincingly to people's thinking and behavior. The central and heretofore unsolved problem lies in relating the importance of film to that of upbringing, religion, education, and many other factors that shape a person's outlook.

Aside from suggesting to film scholars the benefits of a more comprehensive treatment of films in studying the social dimensions of a particular genre, the primary consideration of this study is American history. Public interests, values, and ideas as suggested by the western film provide some clue to understanding the minds of those millions who remain historically voiceless. The film deserves to be considered as part of the nation's transient mythic baggage even as those who care to confront the substance and flavor of American life after World War II consider such evidence as election statistics, political speeches, and intellectual writings.

The mass media are often written off as commercially bastardized cultural outlets that pander to an immature need for escape or easy answers to complicated problems. This is partially true, but it is merely a pejorative form of the more important truth that men can produce and find some meaningful patterning of the complexities of their social experience in commercial as well as individual art. The western movie is one of the mechanisms a democratic society used to give form and meaning to its worries about its own destiny at a time when its position seemed more central and its values less secure than ever before.

CHAPTER TWO

# THE WESTERN FORMULA

B Y WORLD WAR II THE WEST-
ern had become a widely recognized fictional formula. Dime
novels, pulp magazines, comic books, Wild West shows, radio,
and especially the motion picture had created in the Western
an idealized representation of a small segment of American history and a source of innumerable sagas about individual heroism
and social progress. Beginning with *The Great Train Robbery*
in 1903, a newly developing motion picture industry found the
Western to be an ideal format for conveying the kind of visual
excitement and grandeur that distinguished the film from other
media.

Ironically the same scientific and technological advances that
ushered America into the twentieth century also perpetuated,
through the motion picture, a mythic image of the nineteenth-
century frontier heritage. It was the motion picture medium that
most fully realized the mythic power and dramatic complexity
of the western genre after the quality of printed Westerns had
steadily deteriorated during the late nineteenth century. The
movie industry resurrected what Henry Nash Smith considered
an exhausted and socially irrelevant form and made it a truly
compelling and durable popular convention.[1]

Much has been written about the Western, both as an escapist
mechanism for twentieth-century audiences confined to an increasingly regulated and depersonalized urban environment and
as a heroic myth eulogizing America's greatness. It is reasonable
to assume that people were attracted to this often fanciful repro-

[1] Henry Nash Smith, *The Virgin Land: The American West as Symbol and
Myth* (New York: Vintage Books, 1950), pp. 134–35.

duction of a bygone frontier era when rugged individuals thrived in the wide open spaces while serving the needs of an enter-prising progressive society. The Western gave substance to the ideal of personal self-determination and responsible freedom that the realities of modern life and institutions seemed to deny. As modern psychology questioned human rationality and self-determination and as science and technology complicated man's relationship with the elements, the Western offered a clearly de-fined natural order conducive to clear moral choices and the triumph of good over evil.

The Western's idealization of America's frontier heritage of freedom and individualism had its counterpart in other areas of American life and culture. During the same period when western moviemaking began, progressives struggled to reorder America's political and economic life, in part to salvage the individualism that had been endangered by monopolistic capitalism. Wilsonian rhetoric worshiped the small entrepreneur and Jeffersonian vir-tues, while Theodore Roosevelt paraded his rough-rider and western background in the process of introducing greater bureau-cracy and organization at the political level.[2]

By the 1920s the coexistence of modern twentieth-century and traditional nineteenth-century inclinations became noticeably strained as, for example, fundamentalists reacted against the new liberalism in politics and social behavior. Roderick Nash de-scribed the decade as that of "the nervous generation," which sought to redefine values and goals that would accommodate traditional and modern sensibilities. To illustrate the persever-ance of attitudes associated with a preindustrial frontier America, Nash cited the popularity of Edgar Rice Burroughs and Zane Grey, whose outdoor adventures outsold the "lost generation" writings.[3]

Within this changing social climate there emerged from Holly-wood's prolific distribution of Westerns certain definable plot

[2] Richard W. Etulain examines the impact of the Progressive mentality on the origins of the western film in "Cultural Origins of the Western," *Focus on the Western,* ed. Jack Nachbar (Englewood Cliffs, N.J.: Prentice-Hall, 1974), pp. 19–24.

[3] Roderick Nash, *The Nervous Generation: American Thought, 1917–1930* (Chicago: Rand McNally, 1971), pp. 137–42.

types as well as a familiar, classic formula. Frank Gruber's often quoted résumé of plots captures some of the Western's conventional aspects:

> (1) The Union Pacific Story centering around the construction of a railroad, telegraph or stagecoach line or around the adventures of a wagon train; (2) The Ranch Story with its focus on conflicts between ranchers and rustlers or cattlemen and sheepmen; (3) The Empire Story, which is an epic version of the Ranch Story; (4) The Revenge Story; (5) Custer's Last Stand, or the Cavalry and Indian Story; (6) The Outlaw Story; and (7) The Marshal Story.[4]

In addition to plot, the Western was characterized by an iconography that distinguished it from other film formulas. This included elements of costuming and locale to suggest the trans-Mississippi West from the Civil War to the turn of the century. Two major scenic characteristics highlighted the Western's central myth of an emergent American civilization settling an open frontier. First, there was the land—plains, desert, mountains—that both threatened the pioneer society and promised future greatness; and then there were the beginnings of civilization—ranches, forts, and small towns with saloon, sheriff's office, store, bank, and sometimes a school or church—that promised human fulfillment if immediate dangers could be met.

The dangers grew largely from the stretches of untamed nature that separated settlements from each other and from the civilized East. The open spaces were fraught with peril, usually in the form of barbaric redskins and lawless whites. Because of this precarious isolation of frontier communities, the horse and gun were central to the Western's iconography. The horse was not only a matter of life and death to its rider but a companion as well for the journey across threatening plains. The horse also brought settlers to the frontier on covered wagons and pulled the stagecoach that provided a hazardous but necessary link between the scattered towns. The railroad would then complete the contact between wilderness and civilization. The gun was destructive in the hands of badmen or Indians, but it was also a necessary

---

[4] Cawelti, *Six-Gun Mystique,* pp. 34–35.

means of survival when used wisely and well by the socially committed. No Western, aside from perhaps a wild horse story, was complete without the six-gun and carbine to resolve physical conflicts and bring order to the frontier.

Because of the gun's centrality to the Western, the heroes were usually those who displayed an expertise at shooting quickly and accurately as well as the wisdom to shoot discriminately and justly. Behind whatever conflict evoked the hero's deeds of valor were the western badman and Indian—forces that could destroy civilization while challenging it to still greater victories and accomplishments. Surrounding the hero and giving purpose to his deadly encounters with evil elements were the ordinary people who, though the heart and promise of American civilization, were yet vulnerable in this extraordinary environment. The western heroine, usually a refined Easterner or spirited rancher's daughter, exemplified both the virtuous moral fiber of the good community and its susceptibility to physical danger. The final union of hero and heroine in many Westerns insured the spiritual strength and physical durability of American society.

The setting of the trans-Mississippi West during the last half of the nineteenth century provided a historically rich and exciting backdrop for such a powerful and durable evocation of the American heritage as the Western came to represent. If such realities as the despoliation of nature's bounty and the destruction of the Indian prick contemporary sensibilities, the no less real triumph over vast and formidable continental stretches has always elicited a sense of national pride and accomplishment.

Because Westerns suggested the finality, as well as the process, of frontier expansion during the late nineteenth century, they invariably contained an element of poignance that is usually implicit but is occasionally expressed. In its classic form, the Western depicted the heroic interlude that ushered in the good society; but it also conjured a time and setting for exciting and important events that were obviously a thing of the past. The format of a once great but bygone era gave the Western a tone little different from that of Frederick Jackson Turner, who announced that the frontier had ended and with it the source of America's greatness.

Years earlier James Fenimore Cooper's *Leatherstocking Tales* (especially *The Pioneers* and *The Prairie*) raised disturbing questions about the wilderness's giving way to a civilization where regulations, constraints, and behavioral vulgarities clashed with the natural virtues and instincts of the frontier hero. Western movies, also, contrasted the rugged hero's freedom and natural virtues with the ordinary or artificial quality of the townspeople; but, unlike Cooper, they addressed an audience for whom the frontier was no more.

William S. Hart's *Tumbleweeds* (1925) touched upon the dilemma of the frontier's disappearance and the consequent fate of the freedom-loving individualist in a settled environment. Hart, a weathered but proud cowboy, has dutifully paved the way for settlers to move into the formerly open cattle ranges, knowing that this means the end of the free way of life he and his fellow cowpokes love. As Hart watches a herd of cattle, he solemnly tells his comrades, "Boys, it's the last of the West." The point is not belabored, however, as Hart marries the girl and presumably adjusts to a new life. He has responsibly accepted the inevitable march of progress on the part of society and has sacrificed his personal freedom for the collective welfare. Yet the final visual comment in the film suggests underlying regret; the tumbleweed that has symbolized personal mobility and freedom throughout the film is impaled on a barbed-wire fence.

While other formulas, such as the gangster story, have also examined the meaning of individualism in a society that is necessarily governed by laws and institutions, this issue is at the very core of the Western. What gave the Western its "particular thrust and centrality," in the words of Jim Kitses, was its "being placed at exactly that moment when options are still open, the dream of a primitivistic individualism, the ambivalence of at once beneficent and threatening horizons, still tenable."[5]

At the heart of the Western, therefore, was the democratic

[5] Jim Kitses, *Horizons West* (Bloomington: Indiana University Press, 1969), p. 12. Comparisons of the gangster and western formulas were made by Robert Warshow, *The Immediate Experience: Movies, Comics, Theater and Other Aspects of Popular Culture* (New York: Doubleday, 1962), pp. 127–55, and Colin McArthur, *Underworld USA* (New York: Viking Press, 1972), pp. 17–20.

preoccupation with individual freedom amid social constraint that has engaged so many leading thinkers in America, from James Fenimore Cooper, Ralph Waldo Emerson, and Henry David Thoreau in the nineteenth century to Ernest Hemingway, David Riesman, and Herbert Marcuse in the twentieth century. The Western translated a relatively brief segment of American history into an idealization of socially responsible individualism, of a transitional social order both needing and permitting personal freedom and the exercise of individual power. Within the framework of the Western, a man could do what he had to do with an instinctive natural awareness of right and wrong. Fulfilling his personal code of honor also served society's best interests. Not only was the hero bound by social necessity, but society must embody the hero's spirit of individualism. The Western represented what Alexis de Tocqueville found to be the most characteristic and peculiar of American beliefs, "[self-] interest rightly understood"; the pursuit of individual good would not threaten society but would protect and perfect it.[6] The Western also posited the sadder truth that the establishment of democratic order required the cowboy or gunman to subordinate his personal freedom to the greater good. The cowboy could ride the open ranges and heroically battle the outlaw with his six-gun, but only until the social order was made secure.

Whatever questions and ambiguities about the finality of the frontier epoch were raised—especially with respect to accommodating individual freedom with an imperfect social order—most Westerns ended on the positive note that gross injustices and perils had been successfully overcome. This was especially true of the B Westerns that deluged America's screens in the 1930s and 1940s, with their star heroes predictably and assuredly dispatching varmints who threatened the good society. Even Westerns with a tragic ending for the good badman provided satisfaction in his atonement and the restoration of total justice.

With its vision of heroic sacrifice and a tenuous but promising civilization, the Western passed on to modern America something of that broader mythic quality that Francis Fergusson has

[6] Alexis de Tocqueville, *Democracy in America*, 2 vols. (New York: Schocken Books, 1961), 2:145–49.

argued underlay the aesthetic greatness and cultural relevance of ancient Greek and Shakespearian drama.[7] The western hero was a democratic Oedipus and Hamlet who acted on behalf of, but apart from, the larger society to correct some injustice or moral imbalance in the universal schema. Because of his unique relationship with nature, the Westerner, like his ancient counterparts who similarly transcended the mundane, was able to counter extraordinary dangers that defied ordinary people. He often did so to his own personal detriment, since the mundane social order he salvaged did not always accommodate, let alone reward, his kind of self-determination and stature.

*Shane* (1953) remains the clearest and most self-conscious evocation of this western myth. Clad in buckskin, with a gun strapped high on his waist, Alan Ladd as the wandering gunfighter Shane appears larger than life in comparison with the settler family that welcomes him into its home. Shane finds temporary repose from his violent past, as he works and socializes with the family and neighbors. Yet domesticity is as alien to his heroic nature as is the serene populated valley to the majestic but formidable mountains from which he rode at the beginning of the film. Indeed, much of the visual richness of *Shane* is the result of director George Stevens's meticulous employment of different scenic backdrops to communicate a particular meaning.

As trouble brews between the good settlers and a land-hungry rancher, Shane remains a concerned but passive observer with the rest of the community, until a notorious gunman (hired by the rancher) arrives and Shane is forced to assert his superior stature. A scene in which the rancher and settlers discuss their differences, as the evil gunman (Jack Palance) and Shane silently eye each other, makes clear that the conflict will ultimately be resolved by a shoot-out between these two powerful individuals. Shane once again dons buckskin and six-gun to defeat the opposition and thereby save the good community. Yet his heroic act costs him his niche in that community.

Aside from being badly wounded and hopelessly attracted to the married heroine, Shane has become once again the lone man

[7] Francis Fergusson, *The Idea of a Theater* (Garden City, N.Y.: Doubleday Anchor Books, 1953).

*Shane* (Paramount, 1953). A conventional frontier hero.

of violence who can have no place in the good society. His sad departure that concludes the film reflects the classic Western's dichotomy between heroic, free individualism and the more enduring but constraining social order. The West (and the future of America) belong to the peaceful, ordinary citizen-settler, but it could not have been won without men like Shane.

John Cawelti has argued that much of the Western's appeal grew from its ritualistic familiarity of plot and character: "Thus, a very wide audience can follow a Western, appreciate its fine points and vicariously participate in its pattern of suspense and resolution."[8] An amusingly fabricated fan letter that appeared in a 1943 issue of *Variety* illustrates Cawelti's point: "Heartbroke, I sat listlessly through the picture, mentally bemoaning the fact that someone had changed my favorite story. . . . There's no place for genius in my westerns. I don't want them changed. It's too disturbing. I like the old plot. If the Mercury Players make a western, I'll stay away."[9]

Yet, as Cawelti has acknowledged, the Western has been far from static in the elaboration of its familiar plot and setting. Much of the formula's importance and enduring popularity has come from its ability to incorporate within its broad mythic structure a multitude of themes, characterizations, and perspectives. An obvious illustration of the Western's thematic variability has been the appearance of stories or formats belonging to another genre. Director Raoul Walsh, for example, fashioned the western plot of *Colorado Territory* (1949) after his previous gangster melodrama, *High Sierra* (1941). Walsh's *Distant Drums* (1951), with Gary Cooper leading a patrol against the Seminoles, was largely a remake of his earlier *Operation Burma* (1945), in which Errol Flynn had led a patrol against the Japanese in the Burmese jungles (a locale hardly distinguishable from the Florida Everglades in *Distant Drums*). Westerns have also assumed the format of mystery stories (*Five Card Stud* [1965], *No Name on the Bullet* [1959]), soap operas à la *Peyton Place* (*The Way West* [1967]), comedies (*Paleface* [1948], *Pardners* [1956]), and musicals (*Calamity Jane* [1953]). Not even the horror for-

8 Cawelti, *Six-Gun Mystique*, p. 32.
9 [Daily] *Variety*, 29 October 1943, p. 63.

*Curse of the Undead* (Universal, 1959). The vampire as an unconventional gunfighter.

mula has eluded the Western, as evidenced by the toothy vampires who prowl the frontier in *Curse of the Undead* (1959) and *Billy the Kid vs. Dracula* (1966). John Wayne's commando exploits in *The Sands of Iwo Jima* (1949) or *The Green Berets* (1968) seem little different from his cavalry campaigns against the Indians in *Rio Grande* (1950) or against the Confederates in *The Horse Soldiers* (1959). Jack Nachbar recently observed that the name of Wayne's Vietnam encampment in *The Green Berets* is Dodge City.[10]

Even more important are the diverse implications drawn from the Western's basic premise that civilization supplants wilderness. This diversity relates primarily to how films have defined the values of civilization as well as the roles and motives of both heroes and villains. By emphasizing the good and progressive character of frontier society, Westerns could justify the killing of marauding Indians or demand the lone hero's commitment to that society. Other Westerns posited a greedy, corrupt, or self-righteous society that cruelly exploited the noble savage or clashed with the more honorable nonconformist hero. The Western, therefore, became either supportive or critical (often both in the same film) of the growing American democracy, depending upon how the formula's conventional elements were employed. Character traits, similarly, implied values that were either socially desirable or detrimental according to who possessed them and how the story was worked out in relation to them.

The kind of merit or fault attributed to a character or the larger society is seldom divorced from the broader contemporary climate of issues and ideas. Filmed interpretations of the Indian wars, Jesse James, or Wyatt Earp tend to vary according to the concerns and perspectives prevalent at the time when a film is released. Jesse James's change from exploited farmer in 1939 to troubled juvenile in 1957 and ragged nonconformist in 1972 makes abundant sense when put into the context of those particular years.

The Western's innovative potential and contemporary relevance became most obvious in the decades following World War II. Forced to compete against television's popular western series,

[10] Nachbar, ed., *Focus on the Western*, p. 2.

Hollywood phased out the B Western in favor of more technicolor feature productions and more innovative, topical fare that television, with its tight budgets and weekly schedules, could not afford. Philip French has suggested the impact of congressional investigations, during the late forties and early fifties, on Hollywood's use of the Western to handle topics that otherwise would have proven controversial and therefore unpatriotic.[11] Attacks on American racism and the handling of interracial romance were certainly more straightforward and plentiful in Westerns during that period than in the fewer topical dramas about blacks. Screenwriter Carl Foreman admittedly attacked community cowardice and conformity during the McCarthy period in what became a classic western, *High Noon*. A less disguised form of protest would have been unthinkable at the time; as it was, *High Noon*'s message did not elude those who were concerned about the image of America (and Hollywood). A major producer of Westerns testified at the Kefauver hearings on Hollywood movies in the mid-fifties that Westerns continued to be healthy entertainment and that he had not seen "any change in the western picture, the format, than the first days I made western pictures 35 years ago."[12] This attitude toward the Western, together with the release of socially critical films such as *High Noon* (1952) and *Broken Arrow* (1950), suggests that the western form may indeed have attracted filmmakers who wished to address otherwise prohibitive subject matter.

Some interpreters of film and popular culture have taken issue with the postwar Western's tendency to incorporate contemporary elements that were presumably alien to the classic form and, therefore, were aesthetically detrimental. George Fenin and William Everson, in their comprehensive history of western movies, complained that the new psychological and sociological preoccupations of western filmmakers lacked conviction in a frontier setting and detracted from vital considerations of plot and action:

[11] Philip French, *Westerns* (New York: Viking Press, 1974), p. 13.

[12] U.S., Congress, Senate, Committee on the Judiciary, *Juvenile Delinquency: Comic Books, Motion Pictures, Obscene and Pornographic Materials, Television Programs* (New York: Greenwood Press, 1969), p. 137. Mr. Bobo, one of the Judiciary Committee members, concurs that "most of the scripts [in Westerns] run pretty much the same," p. 138.

In the older Westerns, men acted; for better or for worse, wisely or stupidly, they acted. They didn't ponder, debate, subject their tortured souls to self-examination. And there is no reason to suppose that the pioneers of the old West acted in this pseudo-literary fashion either. If they did, they could hardly have survived and opened up the frontier as they did, even though frontier existence required, and received, mature thought and deliberation as well as determined action.[13]

Robert Warshow, in his celebrated essay on the Western, argues that a Western ceases to be a Western in proportion to the amount of contemporary social or psychological comment that intrudes upon the classic theme of hero battling evil. Warshow defines the Western in terms of its hero, a lone man of honor, whose six-gun, tempered with his sense of justice and rectitude, wins the West on behalf of society. Although the hero acts in the interests of society, he acts alone and by his own code of honor. Matters of plot, secondary characters, and perspective merely provide background for the exploits and character of the hero. An *Ox Bow Incident* or *High Noon* fails as a Western, because a social problem and message remove the hero from the center of attention. According to Warshow, *High Noon*'s preoccupation with the failings of the townspeople lessens the marshal's heroic stature; "the 'social drama' has no place for him."[14]

These criticisms reflect what Warshow or Fenin and Everson thought a Western should be rather than anything endemic to the form. The western genre was never inherently realistic, let alone possessing the brand of realism that Fenin and Everson identified with William S. Hart's films. In emphasizing the hero rather than society, Warshow, likewise, imparted an essential characteristic that can hardly be attributed to the form itself. On the contrary, most Westerns have presented the hero's actions in relation to the surrounding society's needs and values.

Warshow's interpretive schema fails him even with respect to the films he discusses. He considered *Stagecoach* an overstylized archetype of the western form, where considerations of "land-

---

[13] George N. Fenin and William K. Everson, *The Western: From Silents to the Seventies* (New York: Grossman Publishers, 1973), p. 42.

[14] Warshow, *Immediate Experience*, p. 149.

scape, the horses, the quiet men" dominate the story, unlike the social orientation of the deviant *High Noon.*[15] Yet *Stagecoach* actually conveys as much social criticism as did *High Noon.* Ringo's departure from Lordsburg and "the blessings of civilization" at the film's conclusion are as much a condemnation of society's weaknesses as was Marshal Kane's departure from Hadleyville— a point that also appears to have escaped John Wayne when he criticized *High Noon's* denigration of America's heritage.[16] Warshow's argument that *High Noon* lessened the stature of the western hero by submerging him in secondary characters would seem to apply better to *Stagecoach,* where the coach and passengers receive as much attention as the hero. In fact, Ringo does not appear in *Stagecoach* until well into the film, whereas the drama in *High Noon* revolves around Marshal Kane from beginning to end.

Recent interpreters of the Western have fortunately contested the notion that the Western is a rigidly defined formula that filmmakers must revere and not violate with too much innovation. Jim Kitses, for example, doubted whether there was any classic model to which Westerns must conform: "The model we must hold before us is of a varied and flexible structure, a thematically fertile and ambiguous world of historical material shot through with archetypal elements which are themselves ever in flux."[17] Philip French put it more colorfully: "The western is a great grab-bag, a hungry cuckoo of a genre, a voracious bastard of a form, open equally to visionaries and opportunists, ready to seize anything that's in the air from juvenile delinquency to ecology."[18]

[15] Ibid.

[16] When interviewed by *Playboy* (May 1971, p. 90), Wayne described *High Noon* as "the most un-American thing I've ever seen in my whole life. The last thing in the picture is ole Coop putting the United States marshal's badge under his foot and stepping on it. I'll never regret having helped run Foreman [the screenwriter] out of the country."

[17] Kitses, *Horizons West,* p. 19.

[18] French, *Westerns,* p. 24.

# CHAPTER THREE

# COLD WAR–PATH

A MERICAN FOREIGN POLICY was of the utmost importance to postwar intellectuals and political leaders by virtue of the nation's unprecedented international involvement and the nuclear character of military deterrence. The Vietnam War subsequently shifted debate from the issue of how best to respond to alleged communist expansion to the question of America's own expansionist impulses.

At the popular level, motion pictures, ranging from communist-menace films such as *The Iron Curtain* (1947) to nuclear disaster warnings such as *Dr. Strangelove* (1964), illustrated the importance of the Cold War as topical dramatic fare. The popularity of science-fiction films during the fifties has been attributed to society's anxieties about possible annihilation by forces beyond man's comprehension and control.[1]

Less obvious, perhaps, but recognizable has been the impact of the Cold War on Westerns. Swedish critics in the fifties interpreted *High Noon* (1952) as a rationalization of America's intervention in Korea, where an endangered peace necessitated countervailing force.[2] An article in *Sight and Sound* observed an increase in western film production at the beginning of the fifties "As America gird[ed] itself against the possibility of another great struggle."[3] From the end of World War II through the 1950s, Westerns increasingly reflected contemporary yearnings for peaceful coexistence by emphasizing the desirability of negotiating with,

---

[1] Susan Sontag, *Against Interpretation* (New York: Farrar, Straus, and Giroux, 1966), pp. 212–28.

[2] French, *Westerns,* p. 35.

[3] Herbert L. Jacobson, "Cowboy, Pioneer and American Soldier," *Sight and Sound* 22 (April-June 1953):190.

instead of militarily destroying, enemy forces. Peace on the frontier, as in the postwar world, was seen to require a spirit of mutual understanding and forbearance, together with the containment of hostile elements by a flexible and prudent application of the nation's military superiority. With the outbreak of the Korean War, this liberal trend in Westerns was interrupted by a rash of films that advocated total military defeat of an irreconcilable enemy and warned against liberal overtures of appeasement as well as outright subversion by treasonous elements. By 1954, however, the peaceful-negotiation theme regained momentum until the sixties, when Westerns adopted much of the cynicism and dissent generated by America's policies in Southeast Asia.

Westerns dealing with the Indian conflict have usually offered the most direct analogy with the contemporary diplomatic scene.[4] The coexistence of diplomatic and racial implications in many of the same Westerns involving the Indian corresponds with the interrelated diplomatic and racial considerations that confronted the United States after World War II. Proponents of racial equality commonly argued that America's effectiveness as a world power, especially in the "third world," suffered from the continuation of racial discrimination at home. Black American representatives increasingly identified with nationalist liberation movements throughout Asia and Africa. The Western embodied an ideal historical allegory for exploring such a racially charged diplomatic problem. American Indians had occupied a dual status during the nineteenth century, as a racial minority within the same country and as a separate nation dealt with by treaties and military force.

The classic rationale for declaring war on the Indian in western

---

[4] Although this chapter concentrates on Westerns which explicitly involved the nation at war, negotiating peace, or countering enemy subversion, there were other Westerns with implications regarding America's position in the Cold War. *High Noon* (1952) and *Gun Fury* (1953), for example, stressed the urgency of personal and social commitment to destroying dangerous elements; Grace Kelly in *High Noon* and Rock Hudson in *Gun Fury* mistakenly encompass pacifist beliefs that are clearly incompatible with the reality of surviving violent threats to society. *The Violent Men* (1955) and *The Big Country* (1958) handled range wars in terms roughly analogous to contemporary feelings about the Cold War; *The Violent Men* advocated aggressive counterattack against the expansive designs of a tyrannical cattle baron, while *The Big Country* condemned violent means of settling range differences.

films is that of removing a dangerous obstacle to the expansion of a pioneering, civilized United States. The Indian often justifiably fought whites because of broken treaties, an insensitive officialdom, or greedy entrepreneurs. Yet violent conflict was almost always inevitable, in which a heroic white man must courageously subdue the screaming red savage. But once on the warpath, the Indian became a menace that heroic soldiers or frontiersmen must subdue. Raoul Walsh's epic version of Custer's last stand, *They Died with Their Boots On* (1941), typifies this view. The heroic General Custer (Errol Flynn) tries in vain to expose a conspiracy by profiteers to lure settlers into treatied Sioux lands and thereby provoke a war that will drive the Sioux from their coveted lands. Swayed by powerful vested interests, a congressional committee disregards Custer's testimony, and the Indian war begins. For all of his sympathy for the Sioux, Custer must defend the American flag against the uprising. Despite diplomatic incompetence and political corruption, the Army conducts itself gallantly in defending the national honor at the Little Big Horn.[5]

*Buffalo Bill* (1944) and John Ford's first two eulogies to the U.S. cavalry, *Fort Apache* (1948) and *She Wore a Yellow Ribbon* (1949), continued to advocate negotiation with a sympathetic adversary while commending the nation's military heroism in a regrettable war. Coming toward the end of World War II, *Buffalo Bill* appropriately concentrated as much on a just peace for the defeated Indian as it did on showing the failures of peace prior to the war. Bill Cody (Joel McCrea) counters postwar hatreds in the East to assure a lasting peace based on mutual respect and good will. Through the humane aspirations of its hero, the film captured the spirit of generosity that was to characterize American postwar relations with the Axis powers.

The Indian wars in *Fort Apache* and *She Wore a Yellow Ribbon* provided the occasion for valor and camaraderie on the part of the American soldier, but the wars were clearly negotiable

[5] The emphasis of this Western and of *Geronimo* (1939) on the danger of vested interests provoking American involvement in a major war is most suggestive regarding contemporary wariness about war profiteers manipulating the United States into another world war.

and thus unnecessary. In *Fort Apache* the Indians present legitimate grievances related to corrupt reservation authorities, but the newly installed cavalry commander from the East, Colonel Thursday (Henry Fonda), forces a tragic military encounter by his demands for unconditional surrender. In *She Wore a Yellow Ribbon* the impatience of militant younger warriors overcomes the wisdom of their peaceful elders in provoking war.

The most passionate plea for peaceful coexistence came the following year with Delmer Daves's *Broken Arrow*. The beginning of the film establishes the fact that the U.S. is engaged in a prolonged war with the Apaches, which neither side can decisively win in the near future. Sick of the pointless killing and loss of lives on both sides, the hero, Tom Jeffords (James Stewart), attempts negotiations with the wise Apache chief, Cochise (Jeff Chandler). Only mutual trust and compromise can avert an otherwise interminable war.

The immediate impact of this immensely popular film could be seen in Westerns of a lesser caliber during the early fifties, such as *Pony Soldier* (1952), *Battle at Apache Pass* (1952), *The Half-Breed* (1952), and *The Savage* (1952); but until the mid-fifties, the message of peaceful coexistence was far from pervasive. With the North Korean invasion of South Korea in June 1950, just weeks prior to the release of *Broken Arrow,* many Westerns took a dimmer view of Indian intentions and emphasized the need for a total military commitment against a devious enemy.

John Ford departed from the conciliatory tone of *Fort Apache* and *She Wore a Yellow Ribbon* in his next cavalry epic, *Rio Grande.* John Wayne again starred as Ford's hero, an experienced army officer who knows better than his superiors how to handle the Indian problem. In *Rio Grande,* however, Wayne no longer proposes negotiation but fiercely disputes diplomatic restraints on defeating Indian aggression.

Republic Pictures released *Rio Grande* in November 1950, five months after President Truman committed American troops to fight a limited war in Korea. By responding militarily to the invasion of South Korea, Truman had undercut mounting criticism of what seemed to be a counterproductive diplomatic stand-off with the Soviet Union. Mao Tse-tung's victory in China, the Soviet Union's explosion of an atomic bomb, and the indictment of Alger Hiss had lent credibility to charges that an administration soft on communism was losing the Cold War.

By November 1950, U.N. forces, propelled by General Douglas MacArthur's landing at Inchon, were pushing the North Koreans across the 38th Parallel toward the Chinese border. China's massive intervention on November 26 interrupted the imminent victory that MacArthur had promised Truman. Five months later, Truman dismissed MacArthur, whose outspokenness about extending the war to include the Chinese "sanctuary" in Manchuria threatened Truman's policy of a limited "police action." With American forces stalemated for another two years, many Americans blamed their president for sacrificing victory for the sake of preserving a questionable peace with the Soviet Union. MacArthur attacked Truman's policy of limited warfare as the "appeasement of communism" and suggested that "in war there is no substitute for victory."[6]

In this context of public dissension over official policy, the topical relevance of *Rio Grande* is unmistakable. The film opens with Colonel Kirby Yorke (John Wayne) leading his weary troops back to post after the Apaches have once more escaped to safety in Mexico. Yorke and his commander, General Philip Sheridan (J. Carrol Naish), are upset over not being able to counter Apache raids into Texas because diplomatic restrictions prohibit pursuit of the Apaches across the Rio Grande river. Sheridan bitterly explains: "That's the policy and soldiers don't make policy, they merely carry it out." Yorke replies: "The State Department could do something." When Sheridan refers to the State Department being able to write protest notes, Yorke says, "I'll declaim them over the graves of the troopers who are guarding the water holes—three of them face down on ant hills." General MacArthur, in his farewell address to Congress, would sound a similar note of dismay at Washington's failure to support his military offensive in Korea: "Why, my soldiers asked of me, surrender military advantages to an enemy in the field?"[7]

[6] Eric F. Goldman, *The Crucial Decade—And After: America 1945–1960* (New York: Vintage Books, 1960), p. 208.

[7] Ibid., p. 205.

*Rio Grande* (Republic, 1950). A proud victory over aggression after diplomatic stalemate.

The need for U.S. military retaliation assumes greater urgency when Yorke discovers that three separate tribes have gathered in Mexico. "This means real trouble," Yorke tells his men, "unless we can stop them before they cross the Rio Grande." What began as isolated raids into Texas threatens to become all-out aggression. Proponents of a stronger military counter to communist advances, whether in China, Korea, or Vietnam (to save the French in 1954), similarly argued in terms of facing a broader monolithic threat of aggression.

Following another futile pursuit of Apaches to the Mexican border, General Sheridan gives Yorke the orders he's been waiting to hear: "I want you to cross the Rio Grande, hit the Apache and burn him out; I'm tired of hit and run, I'm sick of diplomatic hide and seek." Although Sheridan warns that these orders may ruin his career, Yorke smiles relief at being able to breach diplomatic protocol and defeat the enemy.

The question of intent regarding the diverse implications of *Fort Apache* and *Rio Grande* remains more elusive than does the shift in public sentiment between 1947 and 1950 toward the threat of communist aggression to which these films correspond. Ford has never acknowledged any message in his handling of the cavalry-Indian theme. The screenwriter of *Rio Grande,* James Kevin McGuiness, hosted the first meetings of the Motion Picture Alliance for the Preservation of American Ideals, a rightist anti-communist group with a membership that included John Wayne among other Hollywood celebrities. *Rio Grande*'s premise of destroying rather than tolerating aggressors would thus seem consistent with McGuiness's (and Wayne's) political affiliation.[8]

Yet the military–State Department conflict in *Rio Grande* did not originate with McGuiness or Ford. They faithfully adapted

---

[8] According to Maurice Zolotow, *Shooting Star: A Biography of John Wayne* (New York: Simon and Schuster, 1974), pp. 211–16, John Wayne was not always the hard-line political conservative. He had voted for Franklin Roosevelt in 1944 and fervently believed in the urgency of postwar peace. Wayne produced, as well as starred in, *Angel and the Badman* (1946) to preach his convictions about peacefully resolving conflicts. In this role, he played a gunfighter who is reformed from his violent ways by a pretty Quaker girl. *Fort Apache* (1948) and *She Wore a Yellow Ribbon* (1949) also allowed Wayne to play the man of peace.

the viewpoint from a 1947 magazine story by James Warner Bellah. The film story differs mainly in highlighting the marital tension between Colonel Yorke and his estranged wife. If Ford and McGuiness merely repeated a viewpoint that Bellah had published in 1947, it is nonetheless significant that they did so in 1950, when impatience with Truman's containment policy became a major political issue. Moreover, *Fort Apache* is also based on a similarly anti-Indian yarn by Bellah; but when Ford filmed *Fort Apache* in 1947, he transformed Bellah's perspective into an argument for peaceful coexistence—compatible with the immediate postwar support of diplomatically resolving international differences. Ford's willingness to alter Bellah's cavalry-Indian format in *Fort Apache* suggests that in *Rio Grande* he had consciously selected, rather than deferred to, Bellah's viewpoint.

By reducing the conflict between cavalry and Indian to the question of effective military deterrence of armed aggressors, Ford's *Rio Grande* resembled the war movie that again became fashionable as a result of the Korean conflict. Prior to the fifties, stories about an army patrol engaged in a combat or reserve mission were seldom the province of the Western. This was no longer the case by the early fifties, however, as evidenced by *Little Big Horn* (1951), *Distant Drums* (1951), *Only the Valiant* (1951), *The Charge at Feather River* (1953), and *Last of the Comanches* (1953). Such Westerns differed little from *Korean Patrol* (1951), *The Steel Helmet* (1951), and *Fixed Bayonets* (1951). The situation and characters were much the same whether an army patrol skirmished with Indians or with North Koreans.

*Only the Valiant* (1951) seemed especially pertinent to the contemporary issue of preventing hordes of North Koreans or Chinese from swarming beyond their borders. The film's narrator explains how a fort has been constructed at the entrance of a high mountain pass to contain the Apaches using it as a sanctuary for occasional raids. The camera then records the Apache massacre of the fort, signaling the immediate danger of continued aggression throughout the area. An army patrol must then breach the mountain stronghold and defeat the enemy. In 1951 President Truman was busy countering demands for this kind of preventive action against the Chinese sanctuary in Manchuria.

Despite the political controversy surrounding Truman's Korean policy, no one disputed the urgency for national unanimity in the Cold War. Likewise, countries that had been enemies in World War II were now allies in the name of collective security. Westerns of the early fifties emphasized mutual cooperation for defense purposes in stories about the threat of Indians to a country divided by the Civil War. *The Outriders* (1950), *Rocky Mountain* (1950), *Two Flags West* (1950), *The Last Outpost* (1951), *Red Mountain* (1951), *Escape from Fort Bravo* (1953), and *The Siege at Red River* (1954) had Yankees and Rebels putting aside their quarrel to assist one another against alien savages.

In *The Last Outpost* a Confederate commander (Ronald Reagan) risks capture by the Union Army to save a Union post from marauding Indians. In reply to a fumbling Washington bureaucrat who stupidly suggests allying with the Indians to fight the Rebels, Reagan lectures that to the Indian the entire white race is the enemy. No Indian would bother to discriminate between a northern and a southern scalp. Similarly, the southern hero of *Red Mountain* (Alan Ladd) opposes the use of Indians to fight Yankees. After learning that the Civil War has ended, the hero quotes to his northern love (Lizabeth Scott) the words of Lincoln, "A house divided against itself cannot stand." Franz Waxman's musical score sounds "The Battle Hymn of the Republic" as the film concludes with a shot of the Union flag. This theme, prominent in Westerns of the early fifties, of former opponents who became fast friends against a common enemy was obviously relevant to a country that was seeking national unanimity against communism and defensive alliances among World War II antagonists.[9]

The importance of national consensus in combating communism drew additional impetus from charges of subversion and treason within the United States. The celebrated trials of Alger

---

[9] Westerns such as *Ambush* (1950), *Only the Valiant* (1951), and *Bugles in the Afternoon* (1952) made the same point about social unanimity in the face of Indian aggression by focusing on the resolution of personal animosities.

Hiss and the Rosenbergs publicized the leakage of secret information to the enemy, while the Truman loyalty program and congressional investigations attacked disloyal thinking and actions among teachers, government and defense-plant employees, and entertainers. The country was allegedly being destroyed by forces within as well as without.

In the late forties and early fifties, Hollywood, the target of extensive hearings by the House Un-American Activities Committee (HUAC), did its utmost with films like *My Son John* (1951), *I Was a Communist for the FBI* (1951), and *Big Jim McClain* (1952) to demonstrate its commitment to fight communism on the nation's screens. As Big Jim McClain, an agent for the House Un-American Activities Committee, John Wayne pummels his way through a communist network in Hawaii only to see the villains escape justice by invoking the Fifth Amendment. Here again, as in *Rio Grande,* Wayne's heroic struggles are compromised by legal technicalities. At the film's end, his only consolation is in watching the marines board a ship bound for Korea.

Edward Ludwig, the director of *Big Jim McClain,* had previously used the western format to convey a similar warning about un-American activities. The written foreword to his *The Fabulous Texan* (1947) dedicated the film to the "war weary and liberty loving people" of Texas who fought for freedom against a corrupted government similar to that which currently threatened America. In *The Fabulous Texan,* two Confederate veterans return to their hometown after the Civil War to discover that a power-hungry attorney general (unwittingly appointed by Washington) has established a police state. The heroes observe as the state police methodically abuse the fundamental freedoms of press and assembly. One citizen greets them with the startling revelation that "the land of your birth is becoming a Siberia."

The depiction of postwar totalitarian dangers in *The Fabulous Texan* relates not only to the post–World War II communist challenge but, more particularly, to conservative fears of America's welfare state. Albert Jay Nock, in his autobiographical *Memoirs of a Superfluous Man* (1943), wrote: "What we and our immediate descendants shall see is a steady progress in col-

*The Fabulous Texan* (Republic, 1947). America becomes a police state.

lectivism running off into a military despotism of a severe type."[10]

With the growing hysteria concerning a communist subversion of American freedoms and institutions during the early fifties, spies and foreign agents became a familiar scourge on the cinematic frontier. In Republic's *The Bells of Coronado* (1950), Roy Rogers unravels a plot to sell uranium to an unnamed foreign power. After discovering that the mastermind is the kindly old doctor who brought him into the world, Roy races Trigger to a desert rendezvous to abort the loading of uranium onto a small airplane. In one of their television episodes, the Cisco Kid and Pancho prevent greedy traitors from absconding with a newly discovered mineral that could revolutionize the nation's armaments. Columbia's *Cripple Creek* (1952) has federal secret service agents uncovering an elaborate conspiracy to smuggle valuable gold reserves to Peking. By the end of the latter film, nearly every character of any importance, from the sheriff to the saloon girl, has been implicated. Not only has the town's local law enforcer been corrupted, but even the federal surveyor in Cripple Creek turns out to be a Chinese agent for the Dowager Empress.

In the wake of congressional investigations of the film industry and Hollywood's blacklisting of uncooperative witnesses, Warner Brothers and Paramount released *Man Behind the Gun* (1953) and *Pony Express* (1953), respectively, both of which involve plots to separate California from the Union. In the latter film, culprits smuggle guns to the Indians for use against the pony express, the sole link between California and the Union. As the *Man Behind the Gun*, Randolph Scott plays an undercover agent battling separatist intrigue in Los Angeles. Early in the film Scott narrates off screen that it is "hard to believe the city of angels had its share of unholy activities."

Given the thematic premise that America was severely threatened by treason or external aggression, Scott's character in *Man Behind the Gun*, as well as other western film heroes, valued patriotic loyalty and survival above the more humane instincts that detracted from the necessary task of destroying the enemy.

10 Quoted by Russell Kirk, *The Conservative Mind: From Burke to Santayana* (Chicago: Henry Regnery Company, 1953), p. 420.

*Man Behind the Gun* (Warner Bros., 1953). Exposé of subversion in Los Angeles.

When his two partners question his having killed his best friend in the Mexican War, Scott replies that he would rather have seen his friend dead than labeled a traitor.

The urgency of using subversion against a subversive enemy even at the risk of sacrificing home and family is the theme of *Springfield Rifle* (1952). The film's hero, Major Lex Kearny (Gary Cooper), poses as a traitor in an attempt to infiltrate and destroy a gang that is stealing horses from the Union army during the Civil War. The mastermind of the thievery is a high-ranking Union officer, a living example of treason in high places. Kearny's charade as a traitor creates domestic tension when his wife demands an explanation of his suspicious behavior. He can only tell her: "Until this war's over, I have to do what I think is right, else I'll never be able to look at you—or Jamie [his son] —or myself. Men have to do strange things sometimes that they don't like to tell their wives about."

*Springfield Rifle,* like *Rio Grande,* pictures a military leadership frustrated by political considerations in its attempts to combat the enemy. The film begins at the War Office in Washington, where General Halleck explains to Colonel Sharpe that the Cabinet feels it is undignified for the nation's army to engage in spying. Sharpe replies: "The only answer to their [the Confederates'] espionage is an espionage system of our own." The film later reveals that Sharpe operates a spy system anyway, using Kearny as his chief agent. Victory depends upon the determination of military men like Sharpe and Kearny to take whatever measures are necessary to combat a subversive enemy. The measures taken are indeed severe, as, for example, Kearny's maneuvering a badman into a vulnerable position so he can be killed from ambush by a fellow agent. Such cold-blooded tactics, traditionally anathema for western heroes, are deemed necessary to defeat a ruthless enemy, as Senator Joseph McCarthy was fond of telling the public in justifying his defamation campaign. In the end, Kearny's devotedness to a job that threatened his personal happiness receives due recognition in a military ceremony complete with a flag waving in the background and a proud family looking on.

Such patriotic sentiment ran high in the films of the early

fifties, much as it had in the Warner Brothers western epics preceding World War II (*Dodge City, Virginia City, Santa Fe Trail, They Died with Their Boots On*). But there was a difference: the fifties films promoted a patriotism based less on idealism and good will than on the dirty but necessary aspects of winning the war. Heroism involved performing unusually violent and underhanded deeds that especially dismayed the fair sex. In *Rio Grande* Kathleen Yorke cannot fully accept her husband's having wrought destruction upon southern homes in the Shenandoah during the Civil War; in *Springfield Rifle* Kearny's wife balks at his espionage actions; and in *Last of the Comanches* (1953), a tough Army sergeant (Broderick Crawford) eschews the humanistic leanings of a well-bred lady while struggling to bring her and a small group of civilians and troops safely through Indian-infested land to the nearest post. The sergeant's only consideration is survival against a cold-hearted, savage enemy; and this leaves little room for anything but killing the Indian who is hell-bent on killing them. At the film's conclusion, the sergeant receives a commander's praise for his role in helping rid the country of such a menace to peace as the Comanche chief. As the camera focuses on the graves of his dead comrades, the sergeant says they, the real heroes, would like to know that what they died for was worthwhile. Similarly, Colonel Sharpe of *Springfield Rifle* had hoped Kearny's family would someday "understand and appreciate what he's doing for his country."

*The Command,* released by Warner Brothers in 1954 as its first venture into CinemaScope, presents a still more pointed argument on behalf of the use of exorbitant official brutality in the face of danger from the redman. The hero is not a seasoned trooper to whom killing comes naturally but a doctor who is serving his time with the Army. Under normal peacetime conditions, the doctor (Guy Madison) would be *saving* lives; and even as a wartime medic, his duties would normally be confined to healing the wounded. However, near the beginning of the film, the troop's commander is shot by Indians, and the doctor must assume "the command" and the brutal necessities that go with it.

Responsibility for the survival of his military and civilian charges overrides the doctor's personal scruples about combat.

He thus seeks the guidance of the tough sergeant whose army pride and churlishness about killing savages had initially seemed too abrasive. The sergeant explains that the only genuine way to know the "hostiles" is to fight them: "Well Injuns fight two ways, Captain. When they're runnin' against a little outfit, they go ring around right away and close in quick for the kill. But if they're runnin' against a big outfit like we're tied up with now, they keep hackin' and choppin' away at your weak spots till they wear you down; then they go ring around, and once they get you in a circle, they know you're finished." This analysis of Indian strategy, expressed in rhetoric characteristic of America's assumptions about communist designs, guides the doctor's course of action in outwitting the enemy.

*The Command* captured much of the ambivalence in liberal thinking during the Cold War. While advocating the extension of federal responsibilities in securing the welfare of society and advancing civil liberties, liberals acceded to loyalty measures that compromised freedom of expression and a foreign policy that often allied the United States with reactionary (but anticommunist) countries. For the sake of survival against a hostile Indian, the doctor in *The Command* likewise accepts a course of action contrary to his basic principles. Asked why he accepts the command when he hates killing and even blames civilization for corrupting the Indian culture, the doctor replies: "I've got a uniform and a conscience. Right now the uniform covers the conscience. Tomorrow I'm gonna do something that—that a week ago I wouldn't a thought of doing. And I'll despise myself for doing it. On the other hand, I'll excuse myself by blaming my responsibility to—to you and everyone else—I have no choice. Each of us has to fight anyway he can. A life is precious to an Indian or to us." The doctor proceeds the next day to lead an ambush on about fifteen unsuspecting Indians, killing ten of them.

Whereas *The Command* sympathized with its hero's dilemma and his painful transformation from healer to killer, *Arrowhead* (1953) and *Drum Beat* (1954) were openly contemptuous of humanitarian types, whose delusions of friendship with an obviously hostile enemy endangered the national welfare. In both films a U.S. peace commission is massacred before the government awakens to the folly of what amounts to appeasement.

The appearance of Jack Palance (fresh from his diabolical gunfighting in *Shane*) as Toriano in *Arrowhead* immediately suggests this Indian's evil streak. At the beginning of the film, Toriano is returning to his recently defeated people after receiving an education in the East. It is soon clear that he intends to apply his learning to staging an uprising against his foolish white benefactors. The rugged hero of the film, a civilian scout for the Army by the name of Ed Bannon (Charlton Heston), suspects Toriano's intentions, since he was reared by the Apaches and had known Toriano as a boy. Bannon, however, cannot convince government officials that, with Toriano in their midst, the Apaches will reject negotiation and unleash their savagery in a bloody uprising.

Bannon's warnings to the contrary, one well-intentioned but righteous citizen remains confident that Toriano is his friend by virtue of their having become blood brothers in a childhood ritual. The man is fatally awakened to the truth as Toriano kills him in cold blood. Bannon, on the other hand, is not surprised when his Apache mistress (Katy Jurado) reveals that she is Toriano's spy and tries to kill him. After he disarms her, he blandly remarks that her Apache is coming out. She kills herself rather than suffer confinement, and Bannon (with quiet rancor) says, as he summons an Army guard, "There's a dead Apache in here; get it out."

Paramount's advice to theater exhibitors on how to advertise *Arrowhead* reveals the mentality to which the studio hoped to appeal. The pressbooks they furnished to theater owners contain recommended newspaper advertisements which emphasize that the story is based on military records that unveil the "secret history" of this particular Indian war. They describe the role of Katy Jurado as that of a "sultry traitor."[11] The studio was clearly appealing to public interest in behind-the-scenes accounts of conspiratorial activities.

*Drum Beat*, likewise, boasted a historical account to substan-

[11] Paramount Pictures, *Pressbook: Arrowhead* (New York: Paramount Pictures, 1953), p. 7.

tiate the naïveté of compromise with a treacherous aggressor. The experienced Indian fighter Johnny MacKay (Alan Ladd) warns President Grant against negotiating with the Modoc renegade Captain Jack (Charles Bronson). Grant respects MacKay's frontier wisdom but feels compelled to balance MacKay's opinion against the advice of an obnoxiously pious philanthropist doctor who stupidly blames white discrimination rather than Captain Jack for inciting war. The doctor, appropriately dressed in black to match his solemn bleeding-heart perspective, is later killed, along with other peace representatives, at a meeting with Captain Jack.

MacKay dutifully obeys his president's wishes to attempt a peaceful resolution of the conflict with the Modoc but is frustrated in the knowledge that negotiation is impossible. MacKay sympathizes with the angry whites who have been victimized by Jack's ruthless raids, but he argues against reprisals for fear that three white lives will be lost for every Modoc killed. During a meeting with Jack, MacKay toughly reprimands him for taking the Lost River area in violation of a treaty. When Jack claims that he wants only the Lost River area, MacKay calls him a "two-bit tyrant" who, if allowed to keep Lost River, will be encouraged to take more land. Here was the domino theory and the dread of another Munich appeasement translated into a frontier setting.

Where director Charles Marquis Warren, in *Arrowhead* and other Westerns (*Little Big Horn* [1951], *Trooper Hook* [1957], *Day of the Evil Gun* [1968]), views most Indians as brutal savages, Delmer Daves assumes in *Drum Beat,* as he did in *Broken Arrow,* that most Indians are decent and peaceloving. The good Indians in *Drum Beat* resent Jack's breaking the peace as much as do the whites, but they are without any illusions about Jack's violent character or intentions. In *Drum Beat,* unlike *Broken Arrow,* Daves is concerned with the abuse of the nation's peaceful inclinations that resulted in the appeasement of aggression. There must be "peace with honor," an Army general remarks; to which another replies that such can never be the case with Captain Jack. After capturing Jack, MacKay pays his final respects to the condemned warrior whose fighting prowess had won MacKay's admiration. "But you made one mistake," MacKay

*Drum Beat* (Warner Bros., 1954). The folly of appeasement.

tells Jack; "you forgot that people will fight for peace and even gives their lives for it." As MacKay and his ladylove watch the Modocs return to the reservation, Alan Ladd narrates: "And the peace began among our peoples that lives to this day. Peace that wasn't won by just wanting it, but cost plenty. It left scars. But it showed the country something they had to learn and remember, that among the Indians and among our people, the good in heart outnumber the bad, and they will offer their lives to prove it."[12]

Few Westerns after 1954 argued the virtues of violent confrontation as opposed to peaceful reconciliation of the Indian conflict.[13] Concern about frontier spies and subversion also declined after 1953. Savages continued to threaten life and limb, and demeaning racial stereotypes persisted but usually without the rhetorical flourishes about defending freedom against a determined, warlike enemy.[14] With McCarthy discredited in his televised debacle with the Army in 1954 and the House on Un-American Activities Committee having ceased its investigation of Hollywood, the film industry subscribed almost totally the ideal of peace and brotherhood expressed by *Broken Arrow.* Feature Westerns of the mid-fifties, such as *Taza, Son of Cochise* (1954), *Sitting Bull* (1954), *Chief Crazy Horse* (1955), *White*

[12] Delmer Daves, who wrote, produced, and directed *Drum Beat,* intended an accurate account of the Modoc incident, based upon his research of military records. Having presented the Indian's point of view in *Broken Arrow,* Daves wanted to offer the settler's side of the story, which his researched account of Captain Jack allowed him to do. Like most other writers and directors I have interviewed in southern California, Daves had no recollection of intending any analogy with contemporary problems. Only in retrospect did Daves acknowledge the likelihood of unconsciously fashioning *Drum Beat* according to his assumptions about the Cold War. Interview with Delmer Daves, June 1973, Beverly Hills, California.

[13] *The Man from Laramie* (1956), *Santa Fe Passage* (1955), and *Dakota Incident* (1956) were exceptions to the general trend in Westerns regarding the desirability and possibility of a negotiated peace as opposed to defeating the Indian aggressor.

[14] This distinction becomes obvious when comparing two of director Henry Hathaway's Westerns. *From Hell to Texas* (1958) presented the Indians as marauding savages without evoking such ponderous reflections as voiced by Gary Cooper in *The Garden of Evil* (1954); after Richard Widmark stays behind to hold off the Indians so Cooper and his co-star, Susan Hayward, can escape, Cooper remarks: "Somebody always stays; all over the world, someone stays and gets the job done."

*Feather* (1955), *Comanche* (1956), *Walk the Proud Land* (1956), and *Run of the Arrow* (1957), preached peace and understanding between Indian and settler, while emphasizing the futility and destructiveness of war. Together with the liberal trend in contemporary war dramas (*Attack* [1956], *Bridge on the River Kwai* [1957], and *Paths of Glory* [1957]), the predominance of these Westerns suggests that, with the negotiated conclusion of the Korean War and the death of Stalin in 1953, Hollywood was appealing to a public resigned to a less frantic, if still anxious, policy of containment dependent upon peaceful coexistence with the communist world.

Instead of favoring the experienced Indian fighter at odds with appeasing officials (*Rio Grande, Arrowhead, Drum Beat*), Westerns of the mid-fifties often posed an equally heroic peacemaker arguing against the authorities for negotiation rather than a military solution. In *Sitting Bull* a cavalry officer named Parrish (Dale Robertson) risks his career by defying an unsympathetic Indian agent while trying to talk peace with the Sioux. Whereas in previous Westerns women had usually represented a gentleness and nonviolence that clashed with the rugged hero's responsible use of violence, Parrish's fiancée rebukes him for throwing away his career by preferring peace to serving in Custer's ranks. In *Walk the Proud Land*, the peaceful Indian agent's fiancée initially balks at his chumminess with the Apaches.

Reminiscent of *Drum Beat, Sitting Bull* has its hero advising President Grant of the impending Indian conflict. Whereas in *Drum Beat* Johnny MacKay had been skeptical about talking peace with the treacherous Modocs, in *Sitting Bull* Parrish encourages negotiation. In the spirit of Eisenhower's peace mission in Korea, President Grant agrees to visit the West and meet with Sitting Bull.

One of the most popular western stars of the fifties and America's most decorated warrior, Audie Murphy, starred as the gentle Indian agent, John Clum, in *Walk the Proud Land*. Unlike most western heroes, Clum is a mild-mannered Easterner whose sincerity and kindness toward the Apache accomplishes the peace that had so long eluded the hardened military and civilian authorities in the West. Early in the film Clum tells these

*Walk the Proud Land* (Universal, 1956). The enforcement of peaceful coexistence.

officials that the federal government is upset because "the Army over the past ten years, at a cost of three million dollars a year, has been trying to exterminate the Apaches and hasn't been able to do it." A general among them retorts: "We'll do it if we aren't hamstrung by those that have no experience in the Indian problem." Clum questions the existing policy of extermination, and he relays the wishes of the Interior Department to rehabilitate those Indians who have surrendered "and make useful citizens of them."[15]

Promoting a more benevolent approach toward the settlement of the Indian problem was only one side of the task faced by Clum and other negotiating heroes. Equally important was convincing the abused and proud Indian that peaceful accommodation with the new white social order was preferable to the suffering and even annihilation that would result from a prolonged war. The Indian was usually told that he must accept the fact that he could no longer be lord of the plains. The negotiating Westerner therefore argues a kind of fifties brinkmanship policy whereby peaceful coexistence becomes a necessary alternative to the massive destruction that American military power could inflict.

The Indian's determination to fight and die rather than submit to white corruption and exploitation was admirable but only as long as those conditions prevailed. What the white hero ultimately promised and presumably accomplished was a just and honorable peace backed by the good will of an enlightened American public. This was an offer the Indian should not refuse for his own sake and for the sake of the civilization into which he would, ideally, become assimilated. If civilization had failed the Indian in the past, it was because of white racism and greed. What the hero promised and the films assumed was that the Indian could rely upon a more enlightened civilization in the future. A few Westerns, such as *Apache* (1954) and *Geronimo* (1962), suggested a bleak future for the proud warrior in terms of individual fulfillment; but this was the price of securing the larger social welfare in changing times.

---

[15] See ch. 4 below for the domestic implications of Clum's rehabilitation policy.

The restraint of military power in favor of a negotiated peace, enforced by an enlightened American public and its laws, remained a prevalent ideal in major Westerns of the early sixties (*How the West Was Won* [1962], *A Distant Trumpet* [1964], *Cheyenne Autumn* [1964]). *The Comancheros* (1961) and *Rio Conchos* (1964) reveled in exciting battles that revealed the deadliness of warring redmen but placed the blame for hostilities on the intrigues of white gunrunners.

With President Johnson's escalation of the war in Vietnam, Westerns reflected the increasing skepticism and disillusionment with the direction of American foreign policy. Whereas Westerns of the fifties and early sixties idealized a frontier America struggling to substitute peaceful negotiation for a wasteful and unjust policy of military defeat, Westerns during the latter half of the sixties and early seventies conveyed a more critical and fatalistic view of a violence-prone nation that was contributing to prolonged and ultimately meaningless wars. Many Westerns avoided moralizing on behalf of the Indian and, instead, focused on the dehumanizing and destructive impact of war itself.

As America engaged its troops in the largest military commitment since the Korean War, Westerns again took up the theme of cavalry patrols in combat with the Indian. By comparison with John Ford's cavalry trilogy or the early fifties Westerns about heroic exploits in battle, the Indian wars in *The Glory Guys* (1965), *Major Dundee* (1965), *Duel at Diablo* (1966), and *Ulzana's Raid* (1972) reflect the violent character of civilization's frontier expansion rather than any kind of national progress.

*The Glory Guys* resembled Ford's *Fort Apache* in dramatizing the tragic consequences of an ambitious, egocentric commander who sacrifices his men for personal glory, but it lacked the Fordian context of devoted soldiers as vanguards of a progressive nation. *Fort Apache* concludes with John Wayne's tribute to the cavalry for having lived up to its fine tradition, while Wayne's counterpart in *The Glory Guys* (played by Tom Tryon) sadly observes the deceased remnants of the Indian massacre and wonders "how many of 'em [the dead soldiers] weren't afraid to take a hold of everything that came their way while they could still see the sun." Unlike Ford's soldiers, who live to serve their country, those in *The Glory Guys* desperately grasp at whatever happiness they can find off duty, in the knowledge that imminent death awaits them on the field of battle. The respective merit of Indian and white resorting to arms is not at issue; rather, the issue is the human costliness of war itself.

War with the Indian was just as brutal and without social value in *Major Dundee* (1965). Director Sam Peckinpah, who coauthored the script of *The Glory Guys,* began *Major Dundee* with scenes of Indian atrocities followed by a dutiful cavalry pursuit reminiscent of older cavalry-Indian stories. It is soon clear, however, that savagery is not peculiar to the Indian but also reflects the violent frustrations of Major Dundee (Charlton Heston) and his motley troop of Union regulars and Confederate prisoners. The Indian savagery in the early scenes is paralleled later in the film by divisive flare-ups within Dundee's troop and by the arbitrary aggressions of both this American group and the French forces they encounter during pursuit of the Apaches into Mexico. Dundee's army becomes an aggressor by illegally crossing the Rio Grande and raiding a French-occupied Mexican village to confiscate needed supplies.

The villagers welcome Dundee as a liberator, since he distributes food that had been hoarded by the oppressive French; yet the role of liberator is inconsistent with Dundee's ruthless determination to find the Apaches whatever the cost may be to anyone else. Teresa, a well-bred widow who has devoted herself to helping the beleaguered peasants, confronts Dundee with the fact that his so-called American liberators are little different from the bandits, Apaches, and French who have successively raided the village for their own and not the inhabitants' interests. Her point is terrifyingly vindicated when the French subsequently massacre the villagers as a reprisal for Dundee's raid.

The tragically violent nature of America's handling of the Indian problem similarly characterizes *Duel at Diablo* (1966) and *Ulzana's Raid* (1972). Alternatives of peace seem irrelevant as Indian savagery and an equally destructive American civilization clash in a frontier world of violent predispositions. The Army's defeat of the Indian in both films reflects a superiority of guile and brute force rather than the fulfillment of any higher good.

These pointed western indictments of war and of man's self-destructive nature match the trend in the decade's topical films about World War II (*The Victors* [1963], *The Americanization of Emily* [1964], *Beach Red* [1967]) and the Cold War (*On the Beach* [1960], *Dr. Strangelove* [1964], *Fail Safe* [1964], *The Bedford Incident* [1965], *The Spy Who Came in from the Cold* [1965]), in which the devastating nature of modern war and international rivalry renders absurd national considerations of right and wrong. Much of the criticism in both Westerns and modern topical films is leveled at America's unquestioning use of power at the risk of both physical and moral self-destruction.

The growing dissent among America's youth over the Vietnam War acquired sympathetic expression in *Getting Straight, The Strawberry Statement, Medium Cool,* and *Summertree;* while *MASH, Catch-22,* and—more ambivalently—*Patton* extended the mid-sixties' criticism of war and the military. *The Green Berets,* John Wayne's conservative defense of his country's fight to save the world from communism, was significantly the only major film about the Vietnam War itself. It remained for *Soldier Blue* (1970) and *Little Big Man* (1970), both western variations on the cavalry-Indian theme, to attack in a none-too-subtle allegorical fashion America's military efforts in Vietnam. Ralph Nelson, the director of *Duel at Diablo,* vividly recreated in *Soldier Blue* the horrors of the Sand Creek Massacre of 1864, in which American troops annihilated the men, women, and children of a Cheyenne village. Nelson directed the film as an expression of outrage against not only America's abuse of power in Southeast Asia but also such modern atrocities as those perpetrated in Biafra and Pakistan. News of the My Lai massacre reportedly reached Nelson during the filming of *Soldier Blue* and, to his mind, lent additional relevance to his version of Sand Creek.[16]

*Little Big Man* interprets Custer's Indian campaign as military aggression by a depraved civilization against a comparatively

16 Ralph Nelson, "Soldier Blue" speech, 14 May 1971, Box 59, Ralph Nelson Papers, Department of Collections, Research Library, University of California at Los Angeles.

*Soldier Blue* (Avco-Embassy, 1970). U.S. aggression as viewed during the Vietnam years.

humanistic culture. The Army's atrocities in both *Little Big Man* and *Soldier Blue* are not deviations from standard policy or conduct but rather the logical consequence of such. Chivington or Custer, and not Tom Jeffords or John Clum, personifies national progress. In line with much of the antiwar rhetoric concerning Vietnam, Sand Creek tragically illustrates the illusory progress of an expanding America.

Late sixties Westerns about political turmoil south of the border exhibit the same grim fatalism concerning perpetual war in which human devastation erases issues of right and wrong. Most films clearly sympathized with peasant-guerilla resistance against Mexican oppression but without suggesting their inevitable triumph. In *The Professionals* (1966), Burt Lancaster and Lee Marvin fondly recall the excitement of having fought for Villa but admit that these were fleeting moments in a revolution where good and evil were barely discernible and crooked politicians reaped the spoils. Earlier Westerns, such as *Vera Cruz* (1954), *Santiago* (1956), and *The Magnificent Seven* (1960), had been less equivocal in their depiction of successful freedom fights against oppression.

The destructive impact of civilization upon the innocent, a theme of director Sam Peckinpah's *Major Dundee,* reappears in his *The Wild Bunch* (1969), where vicious *federales* employ the aid of a German military attaché and modern weaponry (the machine gun) in their campaign of repression against the peasantry. The leader of the "bunch," Pike Bishop (William Holden), impresses his outlaw compatriots with news about the recently developed firing capabilities of airplanes. Peckinpah set his story in the second decade of the twentieth century, when mechanization was making warfare a more devastating and depersonalized phenomenon. In the showdown between the bunch and the *federales,* Peckinpah highlights the terrifying extent of man's blood lust as various individuals grab hold of a machine gun. As in *Major Dundee* the clash between oppressors and protagonists serves no social function; there is only death on a massive scale.

The film *100 Rifles* (1969) more clearly empathizes with the liberation struggles of the Yaqui Indians against Mexican *federales* and more pointedly suggests American collaboration with

*The Wild Bunch* (Warner Bros., 1969). The impact of modern weaponry for frontier conflict.

the Mexican extermination campaign. The ruthless *federale* commander is aided by a German military attaché and also receives support from an American businessman who is promoting the interests of the Southern Pacific Railroad.

Not even the Civil War escaped the revisionist antiwar sentiment of late sixties Westerns. While the Civil War has usually been viewed in popular culture as a tragic event in American history for pitting brother against brother, it has also been a source of inspiration regarding the heroism and commitment of those who fought and died for their beliefs. Samuel Fuller's *Run of the Arrow* (1957) emphasizes the dehumanizing aspects of the war but then adds the uplifting note of a nation binding its wounds in "the birth of a new nation." By comparison, *Alvarez Kelly* (1966) and *The Good, the Bad, and the Ugly* (1967) offer no consolation in their vivid deglamorization of war. The heroes, or antiheroes, of both films pursue selfish pecuniary ventures as a conscious alternative to becoming committed in a pointless, destructive war.

*Alvarez Kelly* contrasts the tough-minded but pragmatic alienation from the war of the title character (William Holden) with the fanatic, self-destructive devotedness of a Confederate officer (Richard Widmark). Kelly's cynicism and detachment from national causes reflects a sensible regard for personal survival, while the officer becomes physically maimed (losing an eye and a lung) and emotionally callous toward the interests and feelings of those around him. As Kelly remarks after watching the officer burn money he has just earned from a cattle sale, "God deliver me from dedicated men."

*The Good, the Bad, and the Ugly* juxtaposes the unscrupulous conniving for money on the part of its hero (Clint Eastwood) against a background of civil war, where scores of men die for some remote cause. Near the end of the film, Eastwood's quest for the hidden loot is blocked by a raging battle for control of a strategic bridge. When Eastwood dynamites the bridge to stop the fighting and clear his path to the treasure, no one is more delighted than the dying Union commander from whom (along with his troops) the long days of fighting have taken a tragic toll.

Westerns of the seventies continued to depict war as being

devoid of personal honor or national glory. With draft evasion and desertion among the more troubling symptoms of public discord over the war in Vietnam, Westerns often centered on characters seeking to escape the ravages of the Civil War. Jim Brown in *El Condor* (1970), like Eastwood in *The Good, the Bad, and the Ugly,* prefers treasure hunting to military service. The opening scenes of *Macho Callahan* (1970) and *Bad Company* (1972) register empathy for the plight of the deserter and draft dodger respectively. The legendary trapper of *Jeremiah Johnson* (1972) prefers the natural hazards of the wilderness to fighting for his country in the Mexican War.

By the seventies, the nation's resort to arms was no longer considered an aberration from basically peaceful inclinations as in Westerns of the fifties but a logical accompaniment of a dehumanizing civilization. The saga of a unified pioneer America fighting just wars or peacefully settling an untamed wilderness held little credence as filmmakers responded to a growing disenchantment with America's conduct of world affairs.

CHAPTER FOUR

# RACIAL ATTITUDES

**T**HE QUEST FOR RACIAL JUS-
tice for black Americans gained momentum after World War II.
Legal attacks on institutionalized segregation, followed by the
activism of civil rights demonstrators and the more militant black
power groups, stimulated public awareness and a gradual political
response toward racial injustice.

The American film industry, like the nation in which it func-
tions, has devoted greater and more serious attention to the race
question since 1945. Several studies have explored the image of
blacks and the racial attitudes of whites as they are reflected in
films, but these studies have been confined to those films dealing
explicitly with blacks, usually in a contemporary setting.[1] Absent
from consideration has been the Western, and understandably
so, given the formula's minimal inclusion of black Americans
until recent years. Yet in its repeated dramatization since 1950
of Indian-white relations on the frontier, the Western contained
implications relevant to the contemporary racial issue.[2] It was
no coincidence that *Devil's Doorway* and *Broken Arrow* should
appear in 1950, at the peak of Hollywood's initial postwar attention to the status of blacks in American society.

[1] Monographic studies of the black image in movies include: Donald Bogle,
*Toms, Coons, Mulattoes, Mammies, and Bucks: An Interpretive History of
Blacks in American Films* (New York: Bantam Books, 1974); Edward Mapp,
*Blacks in American Film: Today and Yesterday* (Metuchen, N.J.: Scarecrow
Press, 1972); Peter Noble, *The Negro in Films* (Port Washington, N.Y.: Kenni-
kat Press, 1969); and Thomas Cripps, *Slow Fade to Black: The Negro in
American Film, 1900–1942* (London: Oxford University Press, 1977).

[2] The contemporary racial implication of Westerns involving Indians has
been recognized in studies of the Western rather than in studies of the black
image. See, for example, French, *Westerns,* pp. 76–99.

*Gentlemen's Agreement* and *Crossfire* in 1947 condemned anti-Semitism in America, whereas in 1949 *Pinky, Home of the Brave,* and *Lost Boundaries* addressed the problem of racial discrimination with respect to blacks. *Intruder in the Dust, No Way Out,* and *The Jackie Robinson Story* appeared the following year and seem to confirm the public's receptiveness to a more favorable black image than had been offered by a Stepin Fetchit or Butterfly McQueen.

The only Western to handle the black awareness theme at this time was *Stars in My Crown* (1950). Juano Hernandez portrays a kindly southern black who is terrorized by hooded vigilantes somewhere in the post–Civil War South. Rather than indict any widespread social prejudice, *Stars in My Crown* attributes the terrorism to an unusual outburst of human greed on the part on one man, who covets the victim's land. The film's director, Jacques Tourneur, lovingly idealizes a rural community where white and black live harmoniously, blacks happily fishing or relaxing on the front porch and their white neighbors enjoying healthy, fruitful lives. The goodly minister (Joel McCrea) saves Hernandez from the hooded riders in the final reel by shaming them with Hernandez's purported intent to leave some of them his meager possessions. Humbled, the vigilantes ride away, and McCrea's son expresses surprise at his father's having faked the reading of a will from a blank sheet of paper. McCrea affirms that there is a will—"the will of God." The next morning, as the vigilantes, out of costume, sing joyously with the congregation in church, Hernandez is seen through the window meandering toward the fishing hole.

Thus, the one Western that at this time dealt explicitly with blacks was more a justification of the southern dream of harmonious segregation than a forceful indictment of social discrimination. Yet, during the early and mid-fifties when production of modern black-problem dramas declined, Hollywood Westerns exhibited a more liberal racial perspective through stories about frontier intolerance toward the Indian. During this critical period of legal desegregation by the federal judiciary, the Western became a more prolific and pointed commentary on the issue of racial equality than were the fewer films about blacks. It was only with *Edge of the City* (1957), *Island in the Sun* (1957), and especially *The Defiant Ones* (1958) that Hollywood again significantly probed the racial question with respect to black Americans.[3]

Given the atmosphere of suspicion and recrimination surrounding congressional inquiries of Hollywood's alleged "un-American" activities during the early fifties, overt criticism of modern racial injustice would have involved considerable risk. Yet Hollywood could and did criticize frontier America's racial intolerance toward the Indian. This was not necessarily an intentional ploy to disguise contemporary social criticism in frontier trappings, but a fashioning of an established part of the western story in terms with which a contemporary audience could identify.

Treatment of racial conflict in a frontier setting not only distanced a sensitive issue from contemporary reality but also offered the decided advantage of casting big-name stars. Robert Taylor, Rock Hudson, Victor Mature, or Burt Lancaster could play the racial protagonist in a sufficiently credible and attractive manner that would elicit a sympathetic response to the Indian's plight. In the case of Burt Lancaster playing the warrior Massai in *Apache* (1954), United Artists was quick to point out to the exhibitors that many Indians had eyes every bit as blue as Lancaster's.[4]

From the hopeful integrationist sentiment of *Broken Arrow* (1950) to the despairing indictment of *Little Big Man* (1970), the Western's increasing emphasis on frontier discrimination against the Indian paralleled growing contemporary sensitivity about social injustice toward blacks. In 1973 the militant demonstration at Wounded Knee and Marlon Brando's refusal of the Academy Award drew public attention to the Indian, but for audiences of the fifties and sixties the racial question chiefly in-

[3] *The Harlem Globe Trotters* (1951), *Member of the Wedding* (1952), *The Joe Louis Story* (1953), *Bright Road* (1953), and *Carmen Jones* (1955) heralded black casts or a leading black player without focusing on the problem of racial inequality. Sidney Poitier's problem-juvenile in *The Blackboard Jungle* (1955) relates more to the problem of juvenile delinquency than to racial differences.

[4] United Artists, *Pressbook: Apache* (New York: United Artists Corp., 1954), p. 12.

volved black America. The contemporary relevance of the Indian theme in Westerns of the fifties and sixties must be viewed accordingly.[5]

The American film industry, from the earliest years of Western filmmaking, had inherited the nineteenth-century ambivalence toward the Indian. At worst, the Indian was considered a brute savage and represented the antithesis of civilized respectability and Christian virtue. His seemingly innate brutality, as evidenced by violent resistance to pioneer expansion, served to justify his extinction. At best, he was natural man living the free, primitive life, until civilization intruded upon his Garden of Eden and rendered him tragically obsolescent. His proud refusal to adapt to civilized ways, together with his childlike susceptibility to liquor and his weakness in the face of a superior military force, spelled his doom as lord of the North American continent.

The Indian as noble savage became a conventional stereotype in Hollywood Westerns, which usually evinced a small element of sympathy and pity for his predicament along with an overriding sense of obligation to remove this enemy to progress and pioneer welfare. Some early Westerns, such as *Massacre* (1912), *The Vanishing American* (1925), and *Ramona* (1928), emphasized the tragedy of the native American's demise; but these films became submerged in the mass production of Westerns heralding the triumph of civilization over the savage.[6]

*Broken Arrow* (1950) thus was not without precedent in its sympathetic treatment of the Indian, and yet it remains significant for having forcefully stated an ideal of tolerance and racial equality that was to become more characteristic of Westerns. The most immediate precedent for *Broken Arrow* was *Buffalo*

[5] Reflecting the interest of the seventies in the American Indian is Ralph E. and Natasha A. Friar, *The Only Good Indian . . . : The Hollywood Gospel* (New York: Drama Book Specialists, 1972). Based on an extensive compilation of films dealing with the Indian, the Friars indict Hollywood for demeaning the good name and dignity of the Indian. They unfortunately weaken their argument by unrestrained polemic and a less than fair judgment of individual films. The authors are long on hindsight and short on historical perspective in their failure to recognize the relative advances made by *Broken Arrow* or *Little Big Man,* for example, in the handling of a racial theme in movies.

[6] For a summary evaluation of early Westerns that handle the Indian theme, see Fenin and Everson, *Western,* p. 282.

*Bill,* released in 1944 by the same studio, Twentieth Century Fox. A comparison of the two films illustrates the differences that rendered *Broken Arrow* such an important advance.

Buffalo Bill Cody (Joel McCrea) was a man who accepted responsibility to his government and aided the climactic defeat of the Cheyennes, even though he had spent a lifetime as their respected and admiring friend. The film's ambivalent view of the Indian is expressed in a mild argument between Buffalo Bill and his wife (Maureen O'Hara). When she criticizes the cruelty of the Indian custom of abandoning the elderly to die alone in the desert, Bill argues that the Indian is thereby merely adhering to the laws of nature, and she replies that it is precisely this cruel and inhumane aspect of nature that civilization can eradicate. The film subsequently reveals the darker side of civilization—its petty greed, racism, and unhealthy city life (a disease related to an inadequate sewage system brings death to the Cody child) —but it assumes that society can revive itself by moving west and adopting the pioneering spirit.

Delmer Daves's *Broken Arrow* presents the Indian culture as a much more valid way of life than does *Buffalo Bill.* Its hero, Tom Jeffords (James Stewart), incurs the animosity of bigoted whites as he makes friends with the hated Indians. He discovers that Indian customs and ways are valuable in their own right, and he strives to reconcile the two races. Jeffords learns that Indian mothers cry for their lost children and that Indian men have a sense of fair play, traits that correspond with the best values of his own race. He falls in love with and marries an Indian princess (Debra Paget), symbolizing the racial understanding and harmony that can be achieved if the Indian is accepted as a human being. Jeffords tells the noble chief Cochise (Jeff Chandler) that each race must change its thinking and conduct so as to accommodate the other.

Director Daves's lyrical depiction of the beauties of the Apache culture and people underline the film's viewpoint that the two races are not so distant from one another in terms of values. Jeffords's courtship, wedding, and honeymoon with his beloved princess satisfy the highest standards of white respectability, an ideal that would be repeated years later in *Guess Who's Coming*

*Broken Arrow* (Twentieth Century Fox, 1950). The search for racial accommodation and peace.

*to Dinner* (1968) with a black-white couple. Cochise leads his people in a most democratic fashion, subjecting his views to a tribal council before making a decision representative of the popular will. His fair-minded but strict law enforcement provided audiences with an ideal system of quick and certain justice at a time of loud complaints about communists and hoodlums escaping justice by pleading the Fifth Amendment or resorting to other legal connivances. When Cochise discovers that, in violation of his word, one of his people is trying to kill Jeffords, he quickly dispatches the culprit with a well-aimed bullet. In *The Pioneers,* James Fenimore Cooper had similarly juxtaposed the simplicity and fairness of the primitive frontiersman's code of justice against the confused idiosyncracies of civilized society's judicial institutions.

The Indian characters of *Broken Arrow* emerge as considerably more human and endearing than those in *Buffalo Bill* or previous films. If too noble to be true, Cochise is far less stiff and stoical than was Yellow Hand (Anthony Quinn) in *Buffalo Bill*. Debra Paget's princess exudes a warmth and tenderness missing in Linda Darnell's coolly dignified portrait of an Indian princess turned missionary school teacher. *Broken Arrow* was additionally unique in portraying settlers and prospectors as mean and bigoted villains, whereas previous films had confined the faults of white men to crookedness in politics, exploitation in trading, or—in the case of *Buffalo Bill*—the crass artificiality of life in the East. After *Broken Arrow* the portrait of the nasty racist in late-forties films about blacks became a staple in fifties movies about Indians.

Whereas by today's standards *Broken Arrow* may appear to have transformed its Indians into model white men instead of doing justice to the Indian's distinctive character, the point of the film is, after all, that no real basis exists for treating one race as inherently different from, and hence inferior to, another.[7] However

---

[7] Friar and Friar, in *The Only Good Indian*, criticize *Broken Arrow* as setting a new trend of liberal catharsis in the treatment of Indians that still denies them any meaningful identity. Philip French writes, in *Westerns*, pp. 80–81, that *Broken Arrow* and its successors merely reshaped the Indian stereotype; "for all the fine liberal sentiment, the Indian remained one of the pawns in the Western game, to be cast in whatever role the film-maker chose."

questionable is the integrationist assumption that the red or black man is basically a white man with a different skin shade, *Broken Arrow* marks an advance in society's grappling with its prejudices.

Motion pictures rarely delved far beyond the surface of any character, white, red, or black. Certainly Jeff Chandler's Cochise was no more contrived or simplistic a character than was James Stewart's Tom Jeffords, although Stewart's role allowed a greater range of emotional display, as, for example, when he reacted to the death of his bride or the bigotry of the settlers. Popular culture has always centered on stereotypes or symbols, some of which are more progressive and respectful than others. Tonto, for example, appeared inferior to the Lone Ranger not because he was more of a stereotype but because of the inferior connotation of the particular stereotype. *Broken Arrow* undoubtedly substituted one false stereotype of the Indian for another, but one which acknowledged a commonality of human worth to those of different races or cultures.

The popular success of *Broken Arrow* encouraged the production of many other Westerns that preached racial tolerance.[8] Debra Paget repeated her Indian maiden role in *White Feather* (1955) and *The Last Hunt* (1956), and Jeff Chandler took another turn as Cochise in *Battle at Apache Pass* (1952). In *The Great Sioux Uprising* (1953), Chandler assumed the role of benevolent white hero as a doctor who befriends the Indians. He assures the chief that when it comes to healing the sick, "I never look at the color of a man's skin."

Frontiersmen or troopers continued to battle savage Indians in movies during the fifties. Yet these films usually avoided, rather than challenged, the racial perspective that had surfaced in the earlier pro-Indian films. Skirmishes with the Indian were either an exciting backdrop for the elaboration of other themes or carried implications relevant to the Cold War.[9] Only *Arrowhead*

[8] Successors to *Broken Arrow* include: *Across the Wide Missouri* (1951), *The Half-Breed* (1952), *Battle at Apache Pass* (1952), *The Savage* (1952), *Taza, Son of Cochise* (1954), *Sitting Bull* (1954), *Chief Crazy Horse* (1955), *White Feather* (1955), *Comanche* (1956), and *Walk the Proud Land* (1956).

[9] See ch. 3 on the diplomatic implications of Westerns. Westerns such as *Bend of the River* (1952), *Ambush at Tomahawk Gap* (1953), *River of No*

(1953) emphasized the innate savagery of the Indian in terms that seemed calculated to rebut the new racial perspective in Westerns. Bosley Crowther of the *New York Times* recognized that *Arrowhead* deviated from the trend toward socially conscious Westerns. "It is plain," he wrote, "that Producer Nat Holt is having no truck with any social ideas."[10]

More typical of Westerns that posed an irreconcilable Indian menace was *Drum Beat* (1954), a film that Delmer Daves wrote and directed, after his *Broken Arrow,* to tell the settler's side of the Indian conflict. The tough hero in *Drum Beat* argues against naïve liberal types who believe in negotiating with an obviously treacherous Indian renegade, but he also defends good Indians against the angry settlers.[11]

Daves's collaboration on the screenplay for *White Feather* (1955) marks his return to the completely pro-Indian sentiment of *Broken Arrow*. In *White Feather,* the white hero and Indian heroine culminate their interracial romance in a lasting marriage, with no last-minute demise of the heroine as in *Broken Arrow*. The integrationist dream flowers as the two lovers ride into the sunset. Off screen, the hero (Robert Wagner) explains that they were married in the Methodist church and that the old chief who is the girl's father would live to see his grandson enter West Point. This is the same chief who was last viewed mourning the death of a son shot down by the cavalry.

Westerns commonly idealized racial assimilation within a military context, just as postwar racial accommodation was first pursued in the armed forces. The Indian's donning of military uniform in a Western was a testament to his willingness and ability to assume a responsible status in white society, as well as to

---

*Return* (1954), *The Tall Men* (1955), *Cowboy* (1958), *From Hell to Texas* (1958), *Thunder in the Sun* (1959) use Indians for the purpose of staging an action sequence not directly related to any racial or diplomatic issue.

10 *New York Times,* September 16, 1953, p. 38.

11 *Hondo* (1953), *Santa Fe Passage* (1955), *The Last Wagon* (1956), and *Yellowstone Kelly* (1959) are examples of other Westerns that show settlers or the cavalry defending against Indian hordes, while simultaneously alluding to Indians as victims of white expansion or racial prejudice. *The Guns of Fort Petticoat* (1957) makes reference to the Sand Creek Massacre but then emphasizes a brave defense against the aroused savages.

society's acceptance of his race. In the title role of *Taza, Son of Cochise* (1954), Rock Hudson wears a military cap to signify his leadership of an officially sanctioned Indian police force. At the conclusion of *The Last Frontier* (1956), Victor Mature proudly wears a military uniform in a ceremony to show allegiance to his own white race after having spent a lifetime living among Indians. As the Indian hero of Walt Disney's *Tonka* (1958), San Mineo accepts an army uniform for participation in a ceremony to commemorate the tragedy of Custer's defeat. It is significant that *Sergeant Rutledge* (1960), the first Western since *Stars in My Crown* (1950) to cast blacks as the victims of prejudice, did so in the context of loyal military service.

Military affiliation as a symbol of racial accommodation is also related to the commonly used argument that Americans, regardless of their race, deserved equitable treatment in civilian life because of their service in World War II and in the Korean War. *Devil's Doorway* (1950) clearly evokes this rationale in its story of a decorated Civil War hero who loses his land because he is Indian. He, like the black veteran of the 1940s and 1950s, has earned recognition as a first-class citizen and should be treated as such.

*Walk the Proud Land* (1956) condemns racial bigotry in the manner of other fifties Westerns, but elaborates an accommodationist ideal similar to Booker T. Washington's program for the advancement of blacks. Audie Murphy as the gentle and humane Indian agent John Clum teaches the Indians on his San Carlos reservation how to prepare themselves to earn acceptance in white society. He tells a beautiful Indian maiden (Anne Bancroft) and her son to cut their hair in deference to white tastes. He teaches the surrendered Apache men how to establish their own businesses and system of local government as a means of adapting to the new civilized order. *Walk the Proud Land* conveys both the sincerity of liberal hopes for racial justice and the premise that Indian (or black) fulfillment comes through conformity to white ways.

The continued popularity of this integrationist theme in Westerns through the mid-fifties suggests a widespread awareness of racial inequality in America and advocacy of the integrationist concept, at least as an abstract ideal divorced from an immediate contemporary situation. It is one thing to accept a western hero's marrying an Indian (especially in the form of a Debra Paget) or otherwise paving the way for racial togetherness, but quite another to welcome a black into the family or enforce integrated housing. The more liberal racial sentiment in films nevertheless reflects a changing perspective about the race problem and a willingness to consider, however abstractly, the desirability of extending justice and equality to those of another race.

Not every Western during the fifties addressed social injustice with the optimism of *Broken Arrow* or *Walk the Proud Land.* No Western of the fifties was more uncompromising in its indictment of white civilization than was Robert Aldrich's *Apache* (1954). Based upon a novel by Paul Wellman, the film tells of an Apache warrior, Massai (Burt Lancaster), who waged a one-man guerrilla war against the military rather than surrender to the confines of a reservation. Early in the film Massai is persuaded by another Apache to try farming as a means of survival in the new order. But military authorities and an avaricious railroad promoter force a violent confrontation. Massai outfights the Army but then lays down his arms out of love for his wife, who is with child. His surrender signifies not happy accommodation but the tragic fate of a nonconformist in an oppressive society.

United Artists' promotional material for *Apache* quite accurately describes the film as avoiding the usual cliché of blaming the Indian's fate on a few whiskey- or gun-traders instead of coming to grips with the real issue of the Indian as victim of "the inexorable march of the white man's civilization."[12] Aldrich provides an unsettling glimpse of that civilization in a sequence where Massai escapes from a train that is carrying him to captivity in Florida. He finds himself in the bustling city of St. Louis, dodging heavy vehicular traffic and nearly being run down by a fire wagon. He walks by a restaurant, a shoeshine stand, and a Chinese laundry, all three of which suggest to Massai the class society of master and servant that awaits him. He is soon recognized as a "dirty redskin" and narrowly escapes from a frenzied mob.

*The Broken Lance,* which was also released in 1954, combines

---

12 United Artists, *Pressbook: Apache,* p. 18.

*Apache* (United Artists, 1954). The bitter taste of white supremacy.

some of the doubt conveyed by *Apache* regarding the benefits of civilization with the romantic interracial notions of *Broken Arrow*. The film contrasts the snobbish racist bigotry exhibited by the new eastern-style commercial establishment with the respectful generosity shown the Indian by the frontier cattleman, thus suggesting that racial prejudice accompanied the progress of civilization.

Cattle baron Matt Devereaux (Spencer Tracy) of *The Broken Lance* wages a losing battle against a powerful mining corporation that is contaminating his water resources. He goes for legal advice to the man he once made governor and is told to keep his half-breed son (Robert Wagner) away from the governor's eastern-educated daughter (Jean Peters). Devereaux strongly rebukes the ingrate for this slur on his Indian wife and his son, and he gives his blessing to the blossoming romance.

The son, Joe, tells his future bride that theirs will not be an easy road. He explains how the town respectables call his mother *Señora* to disguise their socializing with a squaw. When Matt Devereaux dies, his wife, no longer wishing or allowed to integrate with her husband's associates, returns to her people. Some years later Joe is appalled to find her humbly clothed, as befits an outcast Indian, rather than as the great lady she really is. The film implies, also, that other Indians for whom Devereaux had provided a haven had been abandoned by an unconcerned society. At film's end the mother watches as her son and his bride ride away to face a hostile world.

*Apache* and *The Broken Lance* are exceptionally critical among the Westerns issued at the time when *Brown vs. Board of Education* encouraged liberal hopes for eventual integration. Not until two years later did the more critical outlook take hold with such films as *Reprisal* (1956), *The Last Hunt* (1956), *Run of the Arrow* (1957), and—to a lesser degree—*The Searchers* (1956) and *The Last Frontier* (1956). These films appeared at a time when stiff southern resistance to the Supreme Court's desegregation order raised doubts about the effectiveness of a legal proclamation in combating a deeply rooted racial prejudice. Recognition by blacks that racism in the South had eluded a purely legal approach influenced their use of such direct

action techniques as the bus boycotts in Montgomery, Talla-
hassee, and Birmingham between 1955 and 1957. It seemed clear
that a large portion of white society was not ready to accept
those of another race; and Westerns, accordingly, became more
critical in evaluating the country's propensity for racial understanding. Social criticism in films like *Reprisal, The Last Frontier,*
and *Run of the Arrow* took the form of explorations into the
problem of divided racial loyalties; but the dilemma of racial
affiliation had appeared even earlier, in *The Savage* (1952).

As *The Savage* Warbonnet, Charlton Heston portrays a white
man raised from childhood by Indian captors. He renounces his
white heritage in favor of his adopted race and encourages Indian
defiance of whites for violating a treaty. During a visit to an
army post, he momentarily longs for the refinements of his former
race (e.g., house and Bible), but he is repulsed by the bigotry
of whites and appears all the more determined to aid the Indian
cause. His dilemma grows, however, when he must decide whether
or not to help save a group of white settlers including the white
woman he loves from an Indian attack. He chooses with great
reluctance to save the settlers and almost loses his life in their
defense.

*Reprisal,* based on a novel about the lynching of a black in
contemporary Georgia, offers the clearest evidence of filmmakers
exploring racial questions within the Western genre. In its review
of the film, *Newsweek* observed that Columbia Pictures had taken
"less than civil liberties" with Arthur Gordon's novel: "the time
had been moved back 75 years, the locale shifted to Oklahoma,
the victims turned into Indians."[13]

The half-breed hero of *Reprisal* (Guy Madison) passes for
white in a town ruled by a group of corrupt and bigoted ranchers
whose idea of a good time is getting drunk and raising hell with
a nearby segregated Indian town. He refuses to help his own
people for fear of revealing his racial identity and thus losing
an opportunity to attain some measure of security and social
status by buying a ranch. His grandfather, who urges him to return to his own people, he calls a "stupid old Indian"; and, for

[13] *Newsweek,* 19 November 1956, pp. 134–36.

fear of what others will think, he tells him to stay away. The town finally discovers the hero's identity, and an angry mob nearly hangs him for a crime he did not commit. When his grandfather is murdered, he avenges his death and dispatches the tyrannical elements of the town.

The film concludes with the half-breed leaving the community after the sheriff has relayed to him the town's wish that he return someday when, hopefully, the law will have changed to allow Indians to purchase land. The hero rides off with the white woman he loves, sadly resigned to the fact that society cannot yet accept him "as a man." He must face the kind of discrimination which, according to W. E. B. DuBois, prevented blacks from being "both Negro and an American, without being cursed and spit upon by his fellows, without having the doors of Opportunity closed roughly in his face."[14]

Although Victor Mature's untamed mountain man, Jed Cooper, in Anthony Mann's *The Last Frontier* is white, at the outset he is more Indian than white in sympathy and lifestyle. Through this character, Mann took aim at some of the hypocrisies and irrational behavior associated with "civilized" values. The designs of an ambitious military commander to annihilate the Indians, together with the inhibiting nature of civilized rules and manners, lead Cooper to have second thoughts about living with the white man; but he does finally accept a responsible role within white society. The last scene, with Cooper in uniform saluting the flag, seems inconsistent with the film's vivid contrast between the cruel and oppressive character of civilization and his own honest (if sometimes brutish) simplicity.

In *Run of the Arrow,* writer-director Samuel Fuller presents the most grim and tortured western hero in this vein. O'Meara (Rod Steiger) is an embittered Confederate veteran who continues his personal rebellion against the Yankees by joining a tribe of Sioux Indians who likewise resist accommodation with the United States. He finds love and temporary happiness with the Sioux but soon discovers that they have a cruel and violent streak equal to that in the Yankees. He finds that cruelty and hatred

14 W. E. B. DuBois, *The Souls of Black Folk: Essays and Sketches* (Greenwich, Conn.: Fawcett Publications, 1961), p. 17.

*Run of the Arrow* (RKO Radio, 1957). Disenchantment with the "superior" race.

seem to be universal traits that render questionable the chances for racial harmony and peace. Finally, in the knowledge that he could never bear arms against his own kind in the event of war, O'Meara, with considerable anxiety, returns to the white race, taking with him his Indian wife and adopted son. Fuller wished no one to miss the point that the happiness of these sympathetic characters is dependent upon the nation's solving its racial prejudices. In lieu of the standard "The End" title, he substituted "The end of this story will be written by you."

Fuller's critical view of America in *Run of the Arrow* partially undercuts whatever hope is implied in the ending title. The opening Civil War sequence of the film reveals America destroying itself on the field of battle, and later the nation proceeds on a violent course of expansion through Indian lands. Unlike Tom Jeffords of *Broken Arrow*, O'Meara joins the Indians out of defiance toward his own race and with little of Jefford's idealism about peaceful coexistence. O'Meara's later attempts to negotiate Indian–U.S. differences are frustrated by racial hatred on both sides. Good people exist in both races, but it seems doubtful that they can carry the day. The headlined resistance to school integration in Little Rock, Arkansas, during the year in which *Run of the Arrow* was released seemed to confirm the film's reservations about the resolution of racial conflict.

*The Savage, Reprisal, The Last Frontier,* and *Run of the Arrow* thematically relate to broader questions of individual identity and social conformity that characterized many Westerns and other films of the fifties. Gordon Gow, in *Hollywood in the Fifties,* appropriately discussed *Run of the Arrow* in a chapter about films like *14 Hours* and *Man with the Golden Arm,* in which maladjusted individuals seek escape from the harsh realities of modern life.[15] The problem of denying one's race in some Westerns is basically one of discovering one's identity as an individual and a part of society. In *Reprisal,* the half-breed hero's anxiety stems from a clash between his personal dignity and conformist pressures requisite for material success. The fact that the white protagonists of *The Savage, The Last Frontier,* and *Run*

15 Gordon Gow, *Hollywood in the Fifties* (New York: A. S. Barnes and Co., 1971), pp. 104–6.

*of the Arrow* eventually accept responsibility to white society does not negate the films' criticism of that society's shortcomings. The major character in *How the West Was Won* (1962), Zeb Rawlins (George Peppard), sums up the viewpoint of these three films when he decides to rejoin white society although repulsed by its cruel intrusion upon Indian lands; he tells old Jethro Stewart (Henry Fonda), "A man belongs with his own kind, like 'em or not."

The darkest vision of the American frontier experience to appear at this time was *The Last Hunt* (1956). Director Richard Brooks pulled no punches in his indictment of America's destruction of the buffalo and callous treatment of the defeated Indian. Brooks creatively uses CinemaScope and Eastman color to highlight the beauties of nature and the native inhabitants whom the white frontiersman had emasculated. The buffalo hunter, as if lost to an uncontrollable blood lust, feverishly slaughters the buffalo herd grazing peacefully in a lush green field. An ugly muddy town with grimy, bigoted people stands out conspicuously against the beauty of the landscape. A storekeeper tells a young half-breed to cut his hair if he expects a job, and the young man is roughed up by grizzly looking characters who call him a "stinkin' Indian." Later in the film, a cheap saloon whore is incensed when a customer asks her if she has Indian blood.

The central characters, Charlie Gilson (Robert Taylor) and Sandy McKenzie (Stewart Granger), become partners in the buffalo hunt. Sandy is a basically decent man who needs money, and the army in its attempt to starve the Indian into submission pays well for buffalo hides. Charlie is an embittered, greedy, unprincipled beast who takes his self-hate out on the Indian and the buffalo. In a moment of drunken stupor, he tells Sandy that killing enables him to feel alive and powerful, like "having a woman; . . . it's like somethin' important is gonna happen—somethin' that can't be changed back to the way it was ever again; killin's like—uh—like the only real proof you're alive." Sandy sees in Charlie a part of himself and, by implication, a part of any man; and he struggles to reclaim his humanity. Through these two characters, Brooks suggests that hate and racism are sicknesses which are ultimately self-destructive, as symbolized by Charlie's freezing to death wrapped in a buffalo skin.

*The Last Hunt,* like *Run of the Arrow,* ends with its somber hero riding away with the Indian girl he loves. Taken in their totality, however, both films cast a dark shadow over the nation's frontier epoch, which emerges less as a precedent for progress than as a presage of contemporary bigotry and violence.

John Ford's contribution to the list of 1956 Westerns dealing with race prejudice is *The Searchers* (1956). Although Ford's vision of the larger society remained basically hopeful, he focused on the fanatic racism of his protagonist. Ethan Edwards (John Wayne), an otherwise noble individualist whose social function is passing as the West becomes settled, is consumed with blind hatred toward the Comanches for killing his brother and family and absconding with his niece, Debby. He is determined, until a last-minute change of heart, to kill Debby for having become a squaw and thus an intolerable stain on his blood line.

Ethan's racism is obsessive and socially undesirable. Not only does he ponder killing his niece, but at the end of the film he violates common civility by scalping the Indian chief who is responsible for the massacre of his family and for his niece's abduction. If representatives of the good community are repelled by Ethan's excessive behavior, Ford nevertheless suggests an element of cruelty on their part when the cavalry and rangers (representing the community) charge the Comanche camp. Martin Pawley, who has accompanied Ethan in the search for his niece, decries the cavalry's indiscriminate killing of women along with warriors. The community's desire for preventive retaliation is not without justification, but to Pawley (and to Ford) that retaliation is nonetheless brutal and tragic for the Comanches.

Central to Ford's treatment of racial conflict is the question of miscegenation. Ethan seeks to kill his niece because she has mated with the Comanche murderer of his family. A vivid scene in which he witnesses the raving madness of white women recently rescued from the raping Comanches leaves little doubt as to what has demented Ethan or why the community dreads the Indians. Ford questions the rationality of this fear, however, by revealing that Debby has been fully assimilated into the Comanche tribe. She appears before Ethan and Martin dressed in Indian garb and at first chooses to remain with "my people." To what extent she is reconciled to return to the white community is never fully explained, any more than is Ethan's final decision to take her home rather than kill her. One can only presume that neither Debby nor Ethan can totally erase inherited familial instincts.

Women in Westerns have generally not enjoyed a happy relationship with the Indian. Despite Hollywood's sensitivity to the racial question, Westerns of the fifties perpetuated traditional notions of an inferior race lusting for white women, notions which Winthrop Jordan and Richard Slotkin have shown to date back as far as the colonial period.[16] In 1915 *Birth of a Nation* notoriously exploited this fear of violating womanly virtue, and Westerns have continued to perpetuate the theme until as late as 1968, when hero Glenn Ford in *Day of the Evil Gun* barely manages to save his wife and daughter. Innumerable Westerns have placed women in the position of preparing to take their own lives rather than suffer the ravages of Indian captors. In *War Arrow* (1954), the hero (Jeff Chandler) goes so far as to instruct a guard to ignite explosives that would kill the women should the Indians capture the fort. In *Fort Dobbs* (1958), the hero tells the heroine that he hates to think of what she would look like should Indians capture them.

In Westerns since *Broken Arrow,* interracial romance has been fashionable between a white male and a red female, but an implicit double standard seemed to preclude a reversal of these racial/sexual roles. *Reprisal* and *The Broken Lance* went so far as to link a white woman with a half-breed, but the latter was very much a white in appearance, manner, and social commitment. The title character of *The Half-Breed* (1952) by contrast is more clearly Indian in appearance and, hence, was expected to restrain his attraction to a white woman in deference to the more acceptable intentions of the white hero. Anthony Mann inserted into *Devil's Doorway* a white woman's infatuation with an Indian; but this was evidently considered safe enough, given

<hr />

[16] Winthrop D. Jordan, *White over Black: American Attitudes toward the Negro, 1500–1812* (Baltimore: Penguin Books, 1969), pp. 136–67. Richard Slotkin, *Regeneration through Violence: The Mythology of the American Frontier, 1600–1860* (Middletown, Conn.: Wesleyan University Press, 1973), p. 225.

the casting of handsome Robert Taylor as the Indian—a doomed one at that—who is realistic enough to shun her advances. Lasting interracial unions were confined to white man and Indian woman until the late sixties, when Shelley Winters rode off with a Kiowa brave in *The Scalphunters* (1968).

Moreover, filmmakers used the theme of a white woman's readjusting to white society (after rescue from the Indians) as a premise for criticizing social intolerance. The intolerance may involve racial discrimination, but it has more to do with society's failure to accept and appreciate a woman who has been strong and brave enough to survive rape. In 1957 directors Anthony Mann, in *The Tin Star,* and Charles Marquis Warren, in *Trooper Hook,* reproved society's intolerance through stories of a white woman's readjustment to social respectability. In each case the woman has borne an Indian's child and has brought down upon herself the hatred and recrimination of her peers. In both films a sympathetic white hero courageously defends the woman and in the end marries her.

Mann's *The Tin Star* was unique in that its heroine defends the redmen as being superior to the bigots in her own race. *Trooper Hook* and subsequent Westerns on this theme leave little doubt that the woman deserves society's respect for having lived through the unspeakable humiliations of her captivity. The heroine of *Trooper Hook,* Cora Suitliff (Barbara Stanwyck), came out alive only because of a strong instinct for survival, reinforced by the birth of her child. She explains that her Indian mate beat her only once, but that the Indian women abused her until she began to look and smell like some of them. As she washes herself and her boy in a pond, she remarks that this cleansing has made her survival worthwhile.

Sergeant Hook (Joel McCrea) escorts Cora and her son to her husband, who refuses to accept the child because he fears that to do so may tarnish his good name in the community. Other townspeople who encounter Cora and her half-breed boy condemn her for having given her body to an Indian instead of killing herself. Cora attributes the hatred of the men to their frustrated lust for her.

While attacking society's racial intolerance in this manner,

*Trooper Hook* (United Artists, 1957). A citizen's contempt for the rape victim and her child.

director Warren also depicts the Indian as a brutish savage. Sergeant Hook, like the heroes in Warren's other Westerns (*Arrowhead* [1953] and *Day of the Evil Gun* [1968]), recognizes the Indian's barbaric nature and is thus able to defeat him on his own terms. In a parlay with Cora's Indian mate, Nanchez, Hook threatens to kill the boy unless Nanchez leaves them in safety. Nanchez respectfully acknowledges to Hook that he must be part Indian to risk such a daring bargain. Hook replies that he has learned to think like an Indian and that Nanchez, because he loves his son enough to leave, must be more white than he thinks.

In the case of John Huston's *The Unforgiven* (1959), society's intolerance is wrongfully displayed toward a woman who, according to the film, is unfortunate enough to have Indian blood. A frontier ranch family suffers harsh recriminations from its neighbors when they discover that their daughter Rachel (Audrey Hepburn) is actually an orphaned half-breed. Rachel is horrified at the revelation and at what might happen should she have to leave the family and become a squaw. Led by her erstwhile big brother (Burt Lancaster), the family clings together in opposition to both hostile neighbors and the Indians who want to take her back among her own kind. The fact that she has been raised and loved as a white person refutes the notion of neighbor and Indian alike that she should be considered a redskin.[17]

In Westerns of the sixties, women captives fare little better at the hands of savages and, subsequently, with white intolerance. John Ford's *Two Rode Together* (1961), Ralph Nelson's *Duel at Diablo* (1966), and Robert Mulligan's *The Stalking Moon* (1969) repeat the theme of a white hero who befriends a rescued white woman spurned by her own race. Ford's *Two Rode Together* offers the most disturbing vision of a society unable to come to terms with its fears of miscegenation. The racial fears that in *The Searchers* drove Ethan Edwards to excessive violence became in *Two Rode Together* a social affliction. In the latter film, the Indians are still savages, especially as suggested by the insanity of rescued white captives (as also in *The Searchers*);

17 *Flaming Star* (1960) and *Blue* (1968) similarly depict racial antagonisms surrounding a family member with a divided racial heritage.

but Ford is more emphatic about the hypocrisies and emotional instability of white society. All three films fault society for a lack of sympathy for what the captive woman has undergone. Instead of admiring the woman's courage in surviving her ordeal, people condemn her for having submitted to the savages. Only in *Duel at Diablo* is there any suggestion of the Indian's sensibilities. The final scene of that film poignantly shows the woman's Indian mate casting his eyes on their son for the last time before being escorted away under armed guard.[18]

Aside from continued references to the Indian's peculiarly savage nature in Westerns about captive white women, most Westerns of the sixties emphasized the cruelty and intolerance of white society that discouraged racial harmony and provoked the Indian to violent resistance. The skepticism about racial accommodation in such Westerns of the fifties as *Reprisal* (1956), *The Last Hunt* (1956), and *Run of the Arrow* (1957) became angrier and more despairing in the sixties, a decade of violent reprisals against civil rights workers in the South, ghetto riots in the North, and defiant rhetoric from black militants. With the possible exceptions of *Cheyenne Autumn* (1964) and *A Distant Trumpet* (1964), Westerns offered little promise of society's correcting its racial injustice. These two Westerns perhaps owe their relatively upbeat conclusions to contemporary hopes for imminent civil rights action by the Kennedy-Johnson administrations. Yet most Westerns seemed little affected by liberal promises and programs, just as the Civil Rights Acts of 1964 and 1965 failed to contain the black discontent that exploded in the Watts and other urban ghettos.

Even more traditional Westerns like *How the West Was Won* (1963) and *McLintock* (1963) lacked the implied faith in the happy racial accommodation of so many earlier Westerns. *How the West Was Won* viewed the Indian's defeat as a tragic inevitability of civilization's progress. While given to an occasional demeaning stereotype of the Indian, *McLintock* criticized the government's welfare approach to helping the defeated Indian. The

---

[18] A film ostensibly released for family audiences, *Against a Crooked Sky* (1975) concludes happily, with a wholesome pioneer family welcoming back from Indian captivity a daughter who bears an Indian child.

hero (John Wayne), a conservative, self-made cattle baron who had once fought the Indians but also respected them, shares the Indians' contempt for insensitive politicians and encourages an uprising to protest the degrading reservation policy. The film ended, however, without indicating the effectiveness of the protest or suggesting any improvement or change in conditions. In *Chisum* (1970) Wayne, again playing a cattle baron, complains of the Indians' confinement to "a piece of desert the government calls a reservation." The Indians in both *McLintock* and *Chisum* suffer less from social prejudice than from petty bureaucrats, whose welfare measures are more demeaning than beneficial.

Just as black activism, whether in the form of militant violent endeavors or the nonviolent tactics of Martin Luther King, reflected dissatisfaction with the official legal approach to racial equality, Westerns of the sixties increasingly assumed the need for Indian militancy to achieve equality with honor and dignity. *Geronimo* (1962) presented the famous chieftain warrior as an angry militant, instilling ethnic pride in reservation Apaches given to apathy under the hopeless conditions of their confinement. Unlike former film images of Geronimo as an incorrigible opponent to accommodation, this 1962 version justifies his determination to keep on fighting until the American public forces its political representatives to investigate injustices on the reservation. The film concludes with Geronimo surrendering to a senator who brings from President Cleveland a new treaty that promises the Indian freedom and dignity. Despite the assumption that the Apaches could henceforth rely upon the government's good faith, *Geronimo* advocates the kind of ethnic pride and need for militant defiance that characterized the growing black challenge to peaceful integrationist tactics of the fifties.

Closer in spirit to the nonviolent protest campaigns of Martin Luther King was John Ford's *Cheyenne Autumn* (1964). Faced with starvation and disease on a desert reservation, the Cheyennes request but are denied a hearing when a federal delegation fails to appear at a scheduled meeting. The Cheyennes must disobey federal restrictions and suffer an agonizing trek of 1,200 miles to their northern homeland before the government takes notice of their grievances. With the tribe all but shattered by the long jour-

*Chisum* (Warner Bros., 1970). Respect for the noble Indian rather than the public official.

ney, the benevolent secretary of the interior, Carl Schurz (Edward G. Robinson), tells the Cheyenne leaders: "You've made one of the most heroic marches in history; you deserve to go back to your own homeland and stay there in peace. I'm sure that the people of this country will understand—will agree—when they hear the facts. Now will you take the gamble?"

Ford left begging the question why the Cheyennes should gamble on the good will of the people or their government. The film's disparaging view of white society and a negligent federal bureaucracy undermines whatever hope Ford may have implied in Schurz's speech. Moreover, Ford seems to suggest through Schurz's comments that the Cheyennes "deserve" their homeland because of their heroic march as opposed to their having a natural right to it; that racial justice depends upon a demonstration of worthiness on the part of the oppressed minority.

Even the faint hopefulness of *Cheyenne Autumn* became a rarity in Westerns of the late sixties and early seventies, a period when hopes for a peacefully integrated "Great Society" withered amid ghetto violence and heated protests against the Vietnam War. The Indian confrontations in Sam Peckinpah's *Major Dundee* (1965) and Robert Aldrich's *Ulzana's Raid* (1972) had no redeeming social benefit, only mutually destructive violence. Peckinpah characteristically interpreted the Indian wars as reflective of man's violent nature, whether civilized or primitive, while Aldrich more interestingly emphasized the inevitability of bloodshed between two totally disparate cultures. Ulzana's savagery, including brutal killings and tortures, is a cultural manifestation, no worse than the spiritual death the Indian suffers when confined to a reservation. It is death which is tragic and evil in a fatalistic conflict of strength and wits that no one wins; and the most prominent cause of needless death is either the bureaucrat who operates by the book or the inexperienced idealist who sees the Indian as noble victim on one hand or as inhuman enemy on another. When an idealistic lieutenant asks an experienced scout (Burt Lancaster) if he hates the Indian, the scout replies that hating the Apache would be "like hatin' the desert 'cause there ain't no water on it."

Most Westerns of this period clearly sympathize with the

plight of the Indian as victim of an irretrievably racist and expansionist white society. Missing is the faith in some ultimate racial understanding and reconciliation that characterized earlier Westerns. The integrationist concept is no longer attractive given the degeneracy of white society. The Indian tribe in *A Man Called Horse* (1970), *Soldier Blue* (1970), and *Little Big Man* (1970) becomes a kind of counterculture that provides the spiritual peace and fulfillment missing in the materialistic and mannered white world. These films acknowledge the barbaric qualities of Indian life but view them as cultural manifestations that in *Soldier Blue* and *Little Big Man* compare favorably with the devastating genocidal tendencies of white society. The social dropout turned mountain man in *Jeremiah Johnson* (1972) discovers that the Indian cruelties he has suffered are part of nature's way in a raw wilderness where beauty and savagery are inseparable.

Dilemmas of racial allegiance no longer plague Indian or half-breed protagonists whose ethnic pride and dissociation from white society are matters of personal integrity and certitude about society's evils. Unlike the heroes of *Reprisal* or *Flaming Star,* John Russell (Paul Newman) in *Hombre* (1967) rejects any affiliation with civilized society. A white man raised by Apaches, Russell lives a quiet life taming wild horses, displaying the long hair and simple attire of an Indian. He refuses the opportunity for social respectability when he sells a hotel bequeathed to him by a foster parent. He is unwilling to compromise what dignity he possesses by conforming to the society that subdued the Indian people. He subsequently denies any responsibility for saving the lives of fellow stagecoach passengers who are stranded in the desert following a holdup. His final sacrifice of life in combat with bandits results from his respect for the decency of one passenger rather than from any sense of social obligation.[19]

The Indian heroes of *Tell Them Willie Boy Is Here* (1969) and *Chato's Land* (1972) like Newman's John Russell are self-

---

[19] Just as John Russell would have returned to horse taming, the young Indian in *When the Legends Die* (1972) rejects the modern white world of commercialized rodeo circuits and returns to the traditional Indian life of wrangling horses.

assured in their contempt for the white man. When forced to kill an assailant out of self-defense, the hero of each film becomes the target of a ruthless manhunt.

In *Tell Them Willie Boy Is Here,* writer-director Abraham Polonsky (a black-list victim of the McCarthy era) dramatized a historical incident involving the pursuit of a Paiute renegade through the deserts of southern California in 1909. Dr. Elizabeth Arnold (Susan Clark), whose philanthropic zeal as head of the reservation disguises a neurotic Victorian mentality, encourages the manhunt because Willie Boy has run off with a pretty Indian girl Dr. Arnold has been personally training for integrated respectability. To the local populace and authorities, Willie Boy's capture would constitute a demonstration of civic accomplishment on the occasion of a visit from President Taft. The manhunt provides Deputy Coop (Robert Redford) a long-awaited challenge to prove his worth as a lawman after the routinized grind of riding guard on a reservation. For Coop, Willie Boy is a personal challenge rather than an enemy to society whom he must defeat for reasons of civil responsibility. Coop shares much of Willie Boy's contempt for society's false sense of respectability; and, only too late, he realizes the folly of the pursuit and that in killing Willie he has killed a part of himself. When the sheriff gruffly reprimands him for allowing Indians on the posse to burn Willie Boy's corpse, Coop replies, "Tell 'em we're all out of souvenirs."

The pursued half-breed protagonist of director Michael Winner's *Chato's Land* emerges less victim than avenging angel in the manner of the superblack heroes of the seventies. The whites who hunt Chato (Charles Bronson) for killing the sheriff (actually a bully racist who forced Chato's hand) are mostly depraved men lusting for Indian blood; their leader seeks to relive the glories of the Civil War. After raping Chato's wife and killing his boy, the hunters become the hunted and are killed one at a time by their angry quarry.

The image of a silently vengeful Charles Bronson righteously eliminating the evils of a corrupt society reappears in Michael Winner's *Death Wish* (1974), where, following the rape-death of his wife, he (this time as a prospering engineer) single-handedly wipes out New York City's undesirables. The similarity of roles, avenging racial militant and avenging bourgeois red neck, in two films by the same director illustrates the mentality and perspective common to presumably opposite political factions.

Several major western comedies, *The Hallelujah Trail* (1965), *Texas Across the River* (1966), and *Dirty Dingus Magee* (1970), contain the older, demeaning stereotype of the savage Indian; yet it is significant that these films purposely poked fun at the traditional western formula, including the standard conflict with Indians. The popular western satire *Cat Ballou* (1965) deliberately took aim at white bigotry in a hilarious sequence in which Jackson, an amiable young Indian who can never convince suspicious whites that he was a baby when the Sioux massacred Custer, fights off some bullies at a celebration dance; the sight of someone's wig in his hand sends Jackson into a frenzy of war whoops befitting the scalping savage everyone assumes him to be.

Writer Clair Huffaker and director Burt Kennedy contributed a wryly cynical comment on the Indian's future in American society in *The War Wagon* (1967). Ostensibly a John Wayne action Western, *The War Wagon* contains an amusingly offbeat portrayal of an Indian by former MGM musical star Howard Keel. As Levi Walking Bear, Keel tells Wayne, who has just saved him from a group of Mexicans whom he has cheated, that he is no "dumb Indian" wasting away on a reservation but one who has learned to live like a white man, taking whatever he can get however he can get it. After negotiating an Indian chief's support for Wayne's scheme to rob a gold shipment from the villain, Keel relays to Wayne the chief's wish that he depart his presence, since he finds all white men offensive.[20]

It was only in the 1960s that Westerns began to relate directly to black characters in the process of providing racial commen-

[20] In addition to Howard Keel, veteran performers Bruce Cabot (*Big Jake* [1971]) and Neville Brand (*Cahill, U.S. Marshall* [1973]) also played worldly-wise Indians worthy of Wayne's respect. When Wayne asked Brand's help in pursuing bank robbers, Brand told Wayne that he would track the robbers but would leave the killing to him, since the robbers might be his own friends; Brand also asked that he be paid in advance, in the event that Wayne should be killed during the pursuit.

tary. Aside from *Stars in My Crown* in 1950 or an occasional appearance of a comical stereotype, such as Stepin Fetchit in *Bend of the River* (1952), blacks remained conspicuously absent from Westerns during the fifties. John Ford broke the precedent with *Sergeant Rutledge* (1960), the story of a courageous black buffalo soldier who is accused of raping a white woman. While critical of community racism, Ford assumed the black's welfare to be dependent upon the good instincts of an enlightened white. Rutledge's fate rests with the good will and skills of a principled white army lawyer. Ford also chose to employ the familiar stereotype of savage Indian when Rutledge defends the white lady from an Indian assault. Woody Strode, whose moving performance lent dignity and poignance to the role of Sergeant Rutledge, was reduced in Ford's next two Westerns to playing a mean Indian (*Two Rode Together* [1961]) and a faithful servant to master-rancher John Wayne (*The Man Who Shot Liberty Valence* [1962]). Like Ford, Sam Peckinpah, in a minor tribute to the black soldier in *Major Dundee* (1965), showed how nobly the black fought beside his white counterpart.

In contrast, *Invitation to a Gunfighter* (1964) has as its hero a Creole gunman (Yul Brynner) who avenges his slave heritage by accepting pay from whites to kill other whites. Ultimately, as the film concludes, the enraged gunfighter, filled with disgust at the evil designs of a particular employer and the over-all corruption of a southern town, destroys the buildings along the town's main street. This vivid display of outrage would become a familiar reality the next year, when black frustrations exploded in the Watts ghetto of Los Angeles.[21]

Hollywood responded to the new emphasis on black pride in the late sixties and early seventies by incorporating more black actors in roles highlighting the dignity and often defiance of blacks in the West. *The Scalphunters* (1968) and the *Skin Game* (1972) satirize the white slave-master mentality and present proud and conscientiously defiant black heroes. Sidney Poitier

[21] Interview with Richard and Elizabeth Wilson, June 1973, Santa Monica, Calif. They wrote the screenplay for *Invitation to a Gunfighter,* which he directed. She acknowledged that the script reflects their concern about ghetto unrest.

donned western garb for *Duel at Diablo,* in which he played a cynical, tough gambler in a racially hostile society.[22] Poitier directed and starred in *Buck and the Preacher* (1972) as a wagon-train scout who, along with costar Harry Belafonte, defends black settlers against evil white southerners who try to terrorize them into returning to the plantations. Fred Williamson, in *The Legend of Nigger Charley* (1972), likewise reacted to white violence with violence.

In 1969, *100 Rifles* attempted, however clumsily, to breach the sexual barrier between black man and white woman through the passionate lovemaking acrobatics of Jim Brown and Raquel Welch. The fact that Raquel Welch was supposed to be a Yaqui Indian did not alter the impact of showing bodily contact between a black male and white female. Otherwise, this Western was refreshingly free of the current trend toward self-conscious social criticism. The film settled instead for amusing irony in its major premise of a black sheriff (Brown) enforcing the law of Alabama against a white outlaw (Burt Reynolds).

During the late sixties, only Andrew McLaglen continued to direct major Westerns that idealized the servant-master relationship between black and white. A black servant in McLaglen's *The Way West* (1967) loyally comforts his neurotic master (Kirk Douglas). In one scene, with tears in his eyes he performs his master's bidding, whipping him that he might be purged of sorrow over his young son's death. The early scenes of McLaglen's *The Undefeated* (1969) recall D. W. Griffith's sympathetic depiction of the noble southern planter's suffering the encroachments of the carpetbagger in *Birth of a Nation.* Not only do planter and emancipated slave bid each other a sad farewell, with the planter leaving his loyal black friend an old family watch as a token of gratitude, but the planter also faces the insulting remarks of an arrogant black carpetbagger who has come to offer a measly sum for the plantation. McLaglen remained the exception, however, at a time when other filmmakers considered it more fashionable to highlight proud and defiant black or Indian heroes.

---

[22] Black actors Ossie Davis, in *Sam Whiskey* (1969), and Roscoe Lee Browne, in *The Cowboys* (1972), also played tough-minded individuals who aided the white hero without compromising their racial integrity.

*Buck and the Preacher* (Columbia, 1972). The defiant black hero.

The one film to offer a Mexican-American as its racial protagonist was *Valdez Is Coming* (1971). Bob Valdez (Burt Lancaster) leads a quiet life riding shotgun on a stagecoach and serving as parttime sheriff for the Mexican quarter of a town. When
a black man is slain unjustly, he requests of the townspeople do-
nations with which to compensate the man's widow, but his request is complacently denied, and his efforts are obstructed with
degrading and brutal assaults by the tyrannical rancher who is
responsible for the man's death. Finally, the heretofore peaceful
hero dons his old Civil War uniform and single-handedly brings
the rancher to terms. The combination of quiet dignity and angry
defiance in Valdez marks a significant change from earlier Westerns, which had depicted Latin American figures as humble but
oppressed peasants, as silly but loyal companions, or as snarling
bandits.[23] Valdez's admission that he once killed Indians while
in the army, until he knew better, also distinguishes this Western
from such films as *Sergeant Rutledge* (1960), *Rio Conchos*
(1964), and *Major Dundee* (1964), which emphasize the bravery of blacks fighting savage Indians.

Many Westerns during the sixties and early seventies make
briefer reference to racist attitudes and actions to illustrate the
corrupt or deficient aspects of white society. [24] But, whatever the

[23] In *The Burning Hills* (1956), *The Badlanders* (1958), and *Buchanan
Rides Alone* (1958), Mexican-Americans suffer discrimination in frontier
communities but are too passive, despairing, or afraid to help themselves until
the Caucasian hero arrives. *The Magnificent Seven* (1960) shows Mexicans as
either humble peasants or bandits. Although the peasants depend upon the
white gunmen for survival, it is clear that their culture offers happiness and
spiritual comfort that the gunmen lack.

[24] While the race issue is not a major theme in the Westerns of the sixties
and seventies, these films commonly refer to instances of racial discrimination
to illustrate corrupt or deficient aspects of white society. *Nevada Smith* (1965),
primarily a tale of violent revenge, begins with a grizzly threesome vocally
abusing and skinning an Indian woman to encourage her white husband to
reveal the location of his gold. An Indian's conspicuous isolation from the
center of a failing shanty town in *Welcome to Hard Times* (1967) further
illustrates the undesirable character of the town and its inhabitants. James
Stewart's kindly rancher in *Firecreek* (1968) risks town gossip to help an
Indian girl who has borne an illegitimate child. In *Death of a Gunfighter* (1969)
the romance and marriage of the marshal (Richard Widmark) to a black
madame (Lena Horne) contrasts with the citizenry's anti-Semitic and anti-
Mexican attitudes. In *There Was a Crooked Man* (1970), a black maid shields

degree of emphasis in a particular film, the treatment of racial discrimination in Westerns had changed significantly since *Broken Arrow.* During the early fifties, racial accommodation in film and society seemed viable goals given the aroused concern of people in both races to correct existing injustices; however, this optimism deteriorated steadily after the mid-fifties as liberal remedies seemed too little and too late a response to the growing consciousness and discontent of racial minorities.

her contempt for the respectable family she serves by feigning friendly sambo manners while serving dinner; but after the family is robbed, she and a black fellow servant plead ignorance rather than help inquiring lawmen. Casual slurs are voiced in *McCabe and Mrs. Miller* (1971) about the abundance of "coolies" working the mines. The citizenry in *High Plains Drifter* (1973) refer to local Indians as "goddam savages" and casually ask the hero if he wants a "squaw" or a "Mex" for his pleasure.

# CHAPTER FIVE

# POSTWAR ALIENATION
# FROM THE GOOD SOCIETY

# H

ISTORIANS GENERALLY AS-
sume that an increasingly homogenized, middle-class America
basked complacently in postwar prosperity while intellectuals and
literary artists bemoaned mass conformity and the loss of individual identity in a society of uncertain values and large organiza-
tions. To Eric Goldman "the intellectuals satirized and gloomed
and warned, and the general public did not listen."[1] A decade
later William O'Neill wrote concerning the fifties, "Materialism
and conformity prevailed everywhere, it was said, though few outside the intellectual community seemed to mind."[2] Cultural critics
and historians, moreover, assailed the mass media for reinforc-
ing public complacency with escapist daydreams aimed at the
lowest common denominator in society.[3]

The relevance of so many Westerns to the problems of racial
equality and the Cold War suggests that popular culture after
World War II cannot be easily dismissed as escapist pap or as
a reflection of public complacency. Nor was the Western's relevance limited to headline issues. Rather, it encompassed much
of the social criticism usually considered peculiar to the country's
intelligentsia. During the late forties and the fifties, western filmmakers revealed a preoccupation with anxiety, alienation, disillusionment, and the search for individual dignity and meaning
in a confused and hostile world. The western formula, by virtue

[1] Goldman, *The Crucial Decade—and After: America, 1945–1960*, p. 305.
[2] William L. O'Neill, *Coming Apart: An Informal History of America in the 1960s* (Chicago: Quadrangle, 1971), p. 4.
[3] See Dwight MacDonald's discussion of "masscult" and "midcult" in *Against the American Grain* (New York: Random House, 1962), pp. 3–75.

of its traditional emphasis on individual-societal relationships, proved especially usable in exploring the problem of reconciling personal dignity with communal welfare that concerned postwar intellectuals. Although motion pictures, including the Western, were primarily designed as mass entertainment and usually provided comforting last-minute resolutions, the subject matter was often as troubling in its implications as the most discriminating of intellectual or artistic social observations.

Westerns have traditionally idealized a progressive America in which the interests of the individual are identified and reconciled with those of the larger society. The hero fought either Indians to establish peace or outlaws to restore law and order for the good of the community. The community in turn acknowledged its gratitude and respect for the hero as he rode into the sunset or settled within its fold. A kind of universal justice prevailed, which often precluded a hero with a tarnished past from total integration with the good society. Thus an outlaw with a last-minute change of heart was often killed at the fadeout, although mourned for his good deeds. A man had to pay for his sins against society.

Andrew Bergman, in *We're in the Money,* attributes the decline of Westerns during the early 1930s to a probable clash between the genre's basic hopefulness and the prevailing mood of disenchantment and defeat. The chaotic antics of the Marx brothers and the uninhibited lawlessness of the gangster seemed more appropriate to a people faced with severe economic and social upheaval. Bergman argues that the Western regained its popularity as the New Deal began to inspire public confidence. *The Texas Rangers* (1936), *The Plainsman* (1937), and *Wells Fargo* (1937) represented epic tributes to a progressive country, while Gene Autry and Hopalong Cassidy led the revival of the B Western, where two-gun heroes could again believably make the country a safer place for decent folk.[4]

Yet the plight of decent frontier folk as portrayed in even the B Westerns of the thirties approximated contemporary reservations about the social inequalities laid bare by the Depression.

---

[4] Andrew Bergman, *We're in the Money* (New York: University Press, 1971), pp. 82–83, 88–91.

Republic's *Billy the Kid Returns* (1938) opens with the famous outlaw (Roy Rogers) helping homesteaders survive hard times and exploitation by greedy ranchers. After Billy is killed, a government investigator (also Roy Rogers) shows up to restore law and order. As a look-alike of Billy, he makes the point that he can use the outlaw's identity to scare off baddies and inspire poor folk, while actually possessing legal sanctions for his actions.

In *The Border Legion* (1940), Roy Rogers and his perennial sidekick, Gabby Hayes, are seeking work during hard times. Gabby is first seen sneaking a ride on a buckboard full of shabby-looking ne'er-do-wells, a westernized version of the nation's boxcar migrants. *Wall Street Cowboy* (1939) has Rogers in a contemporary setting (i.e., the Depression), where he is trying to keep a crooked "fly-by-night finance company" from foreclosing on his ranch and thus putting a lot of men out of work. While the film's western ranchers are barely surviving, New York's rich live in mansions and worry about revolution.[5]

Andrew Bergman's assessment of thirties Westerns as barometers of public confidence in its institutions hardly fits two very popular feature Westerns released in 1939, *Stagecoach* and *Jesse James*. In both films decent people are not so much served as exploited by society's leading elements. John Ford's *Stagecoach* posits an established civilized order that is out of touch with basic human values and needs. In this film the Ringo Kid (John Wayne) and his girl friend Dallas (Claire Trevor) are unjustly condemned social outcasts who can find happiness only

[5] Two other Roy Rogers Westerns, *The Days of Jesse James* (1939) and *Jesse James at Bay* (1941), reflected sentiments and situations characteristic of the Depression. In the first film, Rogers is an investigator who infiltrates the James gang only to find that Jesse, a struggling family man, is taking the rap for a robbery engineered by a banker. Rogers and his partner, Gabby Hayes, at one point pose as ex-convicts looking for a meal, an image of human want associated more with the Depression than with the western formula. The famed Missouri outlaw played by Roy Rogers in *Jesse James at Bay* saves poor farmers from being cheated of their land by crooked officials. The idyllic scenes of rich farmland and water rushing along irrigation ditches closely resemble the triumphant finale of the topical Depression film, *Our Daily Bread* (1934), in which a farming commune has drawn water from a nearby river to irrigate the parched land.

by departing from what the wise old Doc (Thomas Mitchell) sarcastically terms "the blessings of civilization." The major villain on the stagecoach is a banker who is absconding with his depositors' savings, while spouting euphemisms like "What this country needs is a businessman for president."

The film *Jesse James* bears a striking resemblance to the film version of John Steinbeck's famous criticism of depression-stricken America, *The Grapes of Wrath* (novel 1939, film 1940). Both are Twentieth Century Fox films, produced by Darryl Zanuck, and written by Nunnally Johnson. Casting for the two films suggests similarities in character types, with Jane Darwell playing both Ma James and Ma Joad and Henry Fonda playing Frank James and Tom Joad. The James family and other post–Civil War farmers face land foreclosure by invidious railroad promoters in much the same fashion as Steinbeck's Joad family and neighboring farmers are displaced by an unfeeling capitalist establishment. Both the James boys and Tom Joad are driven to lawlessness by legal authorities who serve the status quo rather than the popular interest.

*The Return of Frank James* (1940) and *Bad Men of Missouri* (1941) are similarly critical of a legal order that exploits, rather than protects, poor farmers. When in the former film the governor pardons the assassins of Jesse James, his brother Frank (played by Henry Fonda) reluctantly trades his plow for a gun to restore justice. A young farmer recalls his father's words, "There's no law for poor folks except the end of a gun." In the latter film, the Younger brothers become outlaws to prevent a land swindler from legally foreclosing on poor farmers. When the heroine asks the swindler how he can be so cruel, he replies that it is a simple case of economics and that he cannot be blamed if the sodbusters cannot meet their financial obligations.

Other good bad-guy Westerns of the early forties that capitalized on the popularity of *Jesse James* were less inclined to dwell on widespread social injustice or on the dichotomy between popular and official interests. Attention generally centered on the outlaw's option of either pursuing selfish, illegal actions or contributing in a more legal fashion to the community's best interests.

*Jesse James* (Twentieth Century Fox, 1939). Hard times in the Depression-era Western.

The story context concerned more the development of a progressive pioneer nation than the exploitation of the poor by corrupt authorities.

The prospect of war in Europe may well have influenced the Western's emphasis on communal solidarity and national progress. MGM's technicolor but dull production of *Billy the Kid* (1940) contrasts the virtues of a lawful democratic struggle against a tyrannical land-grabber with the title figure's propensity for arbitrary righteous violence. Billy's rancher-benefactor predicts that the good citizens will unite to overthrow evil elements so as to leave little room for "Napoleons, Hannibals, or Billy the Kids." In both *Western Union* (1941) and *Belle Starr* (1941), Randolph Scott plays an outlaw, whose individual desires and concerns must bow before the good of the state. He forsakes outlawry to help build the Western Union telegraph in one film, whereas in the other he mistakenly pursues his own interests rather than those of Missouri.

Populist Robin Hoods, such as Jesse James, Billy the Kid, or Randolph Scott's Sam Starr, raised the spectre of demagogues when unbridled by the restraints of democratic institutions. The danger of corrupting power figured significantly in most outlaw stories, however justified and sympathetic the outlaw hero might otherwise be. *Dark Command* (1940) and *Santa Fe Trail* (1940) unequivocally condemn the demagogic insanities of Quantrill and John Brown as destructive of a democratic approach to problems of law and order or slavery.

Westerns such as *Honky Tonk* (1941), *Texas* (1941), *The Desperadoes* (1943), and *Barbary Coast Gent* (1943) continue the trend of the sympathetic bad guy, but in a more lighthearted vein. The heroes are more happy-go-lucky scoundrels than tragic figures like Jesse James or Billy the Kid. The depression-oriented social criticism of *Jesse James* and *Stagecoach* gave way during the war years to uplifting frontier tributes to national unanimity. Warner Brothers, which had released so many contemporary-problem dramas during the Depression, became the foremost producer of such glory-laden frontier epics as *Dodge City* (1939), *Virginia City* (1940), *Santa Fe Trail* (1940), *They Died with Their Boots On* (1941), and *San Antonio* (1945). Warner's first contribution to the outlaw cycle, *The Oklahoma Kid* (1939) differs markedly from *Jesse James* and *Stagecoach* in providing its outlaw hero with a background of rousing pioneer endeavor toward settling the new West.

*The Outlaw* (1943) and *The Ox Bow Incident* (1943) stand out as exceptions to the prevailing spirit among wartime Westerns concerning individuals united in a common cause. *The Outlaw,* because of censorship difficulties related to the exposure of Jane Russell's anatomy and the unusually suggestive sexual encounters, was withdrawn from circulation and rereleased in 1946. Howard Hughes produced and (replacing director Howard Hawks) directed this rambunctious and highly fictionalized yarn of Billy the Kid. Instead of the usual serious account of Billy's tenuous relationship with the community, Hughes and screenwriter Jules Furthman concocted a glib series of adventures revolving around Billy's on-again, off-again friendship with Doc Holliday and torrid romance with the busty Rio (Jane Russell). The issue of social commitment never emerges, as Billy remains throughout the film a precociously charming juvenile in need of a friend and bed partner.

*The Ox Bow Incident* provides a grim indictment of mob violence, human callousness, and mass hysteria in a frontier community. A posse of angry, neurotic citizens takes the law into its own hands and hangs three suspected rustlers only to discover, to their shame and self-disgust, that they have hanged the wrong parties. A cowboy protests the hanging but is helpless against mob hysteria. Early scenes of the town convey a sense of the emptiness and decay that afflicts most of the posse members, as if to suggest that mass cruelty and violence emanate from a kind of desperate boredom and repression of human vitality. This kind of social criticism of a community where blind conformity has supplanted the dictates of conscience and sound judgment is unique in Westerns of the forties, but it would become a common theme in the fifties. Perhaps this explains why Twentieth Century Fox remade *The Ox Bow Incident* for television in 1956 despite the failure of the original at the box office in 1943.[6]

[6] As an affirmation of law versus mob rule, *The Ox Bow Incident* (1943) reflected contemporary sentiment concerning the breakdown of democratic order and decency represented by the Nazi terror.

*Tall in the Saddle* (1944), *Dakota* (1945), and *San Antonio* (1945) are typical of wartime Westerns, with strong individualist heroes committed to the social good. Intellectual thought during the war years likewise reflected inclinations toward emphasizing the compatibility of individualist and societal impulses in America. Historians such as James Truslow Adams, Ralph Barton Perry, and Charles and Mary Beard praised the strength of a progressive American civilization that joined the ideals of social responsibility and individual liberty. Adams boasted the ability of Americans to join in cooperative efforts toward the general welfare without becoming conformists. The Beards referred to "individual liberty" and "social principle" as complementary American traits. Perry argued that the frontier experience had reinforced a "collective individualism" originating in Puritan thought.[7]

Margaret Mead, well-known as a commentator on the American character during the war, sought in her book *And Keep Your Powder Dry* to encourage greater reflective cultural awareness as a national means of confronting the foreign crisis more effectively. The Cold War subsequently inspired similar sentiments from other intellectuals who were convinced that victory, or at least survival, depended largely upon the extent to which Americans recognized their distinct strengths and weaknesses as a national group. If Mead was as convinced as were her wartime contemporaries regarding the nation's basic worth, she nevertheless dwelled upon nagging weaknesses.

What bothered Mead about American values became a growing concern among postwar social observers, namely, the incompatibility of certain facets of the nineteenth-century individualist success ethic with the modern industrial society. While some (Margaret Mead, Henry Bamford Parkes) regretted losing something of the personal creativeness, energy, and responsibility associated with the old values, others (F. S. C. Northrup, Clyde Kluckhohn) advocated the evolution of new values more appropriate to the existing industrial order.[8]

[7] Thomas L. Hartshorne, *The Distorted Image: Changing Conceptions of the American Character since Turner* (Cleveland: Press of Case-Western Reserve University, 1968), pp. 139–41.
[8] Ibid., pp. 135–38, 142–48.

A similar difference of leanings characterized the debate between conservative thinkers, who deplored the sacrifice of individualism on the altars of a welfare state, and liberals, who
looked to the practical application of public guardianship (à
la Roosevelt's New Deal) as the best assurance of continued
strength and progress.[9] The totalitarian challenges of both Nazi
Germany and the Soviet Union added impetus to these attempts
to define America's democratic values in a way that would reward individual success while preserving the interests and welfare of society.

During, and especially the half decade after, World War II
major Westerns explored the tension between individual success
(and power) and the collective welfare. The self-made frontier
tycoon usually found himself at odds with the emerging community of new settlers who populated the growing democratic society. The successful entrepreneur possessed vision and ambition,
qualities that had served him well in conquering a savage frontier but that rendered him a threat to the expanding democracy.
These Westerns acknowledged the talents and accomplishments
of the empire builder while stressing the need to reconcile his
power with the democratic will.

*American Empire* (1942) and *The Great Man's Lady* (1942)
pay respect to the great-man theory of inspired individualists who
laid the foundations for a great nation. The cattle baron (Pres-
ton Foster) of *American Empire* and the town builder (Joel
McCrea) of *The Great Man's Lady* identify their personal ambitions with serving the good of the country. There comes a time,
however, when their private interests clash with those of the
common people. The cattle baron (Foster) fences off the open
range to protect his cattle from rustlers despite the harmful impact on settlers who need that range to build their own herds.
After a nearly violent confrontation with the settlers, the cattle
baron recognizes that the country also belongs to "the little man."

---

[9] Selections from the writings of both conservative intellectuals (e.g.,
Russell Kirk and Friedrich Hayek) and their liberal counterparts (e.g., Arthur
Schlesinger, Jr., and Sidney Hook) appear in Chester E. Eisinger, ed., *The
1940s: Profile of a Nation in Crisis* (Garden City, N.Y.: Anchor Books, 1969),
pp. 338–455.

Fences remain necessary, but gates are furnished for "our neighbors," so that everyone can help develop the cattle industry and make Texas the greatest state in the Union.

After building what will become a beautiful American metropolis, the hero of *The Great Man's Lady* lends his potential support to a railroad company that will benefit the city commercially but will also dominate the town. When his former wife (Barbara Stanwyck) argues irrefutably that the town belongs to the people and not to the railroad, the great man switches his support from the moneyed interests to the greater democracy.

Niven Busch's stories for *Duel in the Sun* (1946) and *The Furies* (1950) address a similar conflict but with less admiration showered on the powerful figure. These two films involve aging and embittered cattle barons, whose wars with homesteaders and small competitors threaten equal opportunity and civil rights. Senator McCanles (Lionel Barrymore) in *Duel in the Sun* has become a domineering old curmudgeon since crippled by a leg injury sustained years ago. He rules his cattle empire with an iron hand, browbeats his wife, spoils a rotten son, and casts racist slurs at the half-breed beauty left in his wife's charge. Toward the end of the film, however, McCanles recognizes the errors of his ways and reveals something of the humanity that had disappeared with his leg. An earlier suggestion of the man's inner dignity occurs during McCanles's armed confrontation with a group of railroaders and other citizens out to enforce a legal right-of-way to build track through his land. He says, as he sees the cavalry approaching beneath the waving American flag: "I once fought for that flag. I'll not fire on it."

T. C. Jeffords (Walter Huston), the cattle baron in *The Furies,* is considerably more ruthless than McCanles in his disregard for the public welfare. Yet, when his equally strong-willed daughter (Barbara Stanwyck) finally succeeds in ruining him financially, T.C. takes it like the man he is, acknowledging that his own flesh and blood has beaten him fairly at his own game. As the film ends, the daughter and her beau respectfully bury the old man on his ranch and plan to name their firstborn son T.C.

A more ambivalent attitude toward the conflict between cattle baron and society is projected in *The Sea of Grass* (1947). Jim

Brewton (Spencer Tracy) is insensitive to the poverty-stricken homesteaders and contemptuous of their legal rights to the land he has reserved for cattle grazing. But he is not motivated by sheer greed, and he does not display the vulgarity of McCanles (*Duel in the Sun*) or of Jeffords (*The Furies*). He expresses genuine affection for the rich grasslands, which he correctly believes would be ruined by the homesteader's plow. After the law forces him to allow homesteaders to farm the land, heavy rains destroy the plowed soil and prove his contention that God ordained the "sea of grass" for buffalo and cattle.

The conservationist message of *The Sea of Grass* seems modeled after Pare Lorentz's *The Plow That Broke the Plains* (1936), which was produced for the New Deal's resettlement administration; except that it is Tracy, the successful individualist, and not the public's legal guardians who protects nature's bounty from human waste. Although sympathetic to society's demand that Tracy submit to the public will, *The Sea of Grass* attributes to him a wisdom and strength of character that no amount of law and government can duplicate. The film proposes that no man is above the law or the will of the majority, but it also suggests that a progressive democracy can ill afford to lose the strength and stature of the frontier empire-builder.

Howard Hawks's *Red River* (1948) begins its saga of a socially alienated cattle baron by showing how Tom Dunson (John Wayne) carved an empire with only his vision and six-gun to assist him. The body of the film chronicles the desperate attempt by Dunson, now a powerful cattleman, to drive his cattle from Texas to the new railroad in Kansas. The country's need for beef and the survival of Texas cattlemen require all the courage and tenacity Dunson can muster in accomplishing the unprecedented transport of so many cattle over such a long distance.

Under the weight of this awesome challenge, Dunson's determination becomes a dangerous obsession, to the point where he loses all human sensitivity to the morale and welfare of his men. When he shoots three men and tries to hang two others for deserting the cattle drive, his adopted son Matthew Garth (Montgomery Clift) usurps command. Garth possesses his guardian's courage and the skill to complete the cattle drive but without

*Red River* (United Artists, 1948). The enterprising tycoon insensitive to the good of society.

Dunson's tyrannical streak. After the two confront each other in a suspenseful showdown, Dunson recognizes his own obsessive behavior and is reconciled with Garth and the greater good. Tom Dunson's individualism has become, like Matthew Garth's, tempered with the social sensitivity vital to a growing democratic community.

A variation of the cattle baron at odds with the social welfare is Errol Flynn's silver-mining tycoon in *Silver River* (1948). True to format, Mike McComb (Flynn) eventually succumbs to the will of the majority by aligning himself with the popular interest, but only after an hour and a half of arrogant opportunism.

McComb's selfish behavior masks his bitterness at having been unfairly discharged from the Army for alleged misconduct. As with Tom Dunson in *Red River,* McComb is obsessed with avenging an injury to his pride. In addition, he expresses determination to make his mark on the world rather than remain one of the anonymous masses. In its hero's fear of anonymity, *Silver River* touches upon an important concern of postwar intellectuals: modern man's anxieties over the loss of personal identity in a mass society. While arguing that these anxieties eventually encourage conformity in America's competitive society, psychologists like Karen Horney and Erich Fromm acknowledged the success drive by which modern man (like McComb) hopes to escape an anonymous existence.[10]

*Silver River* is one of many Westerns that, from the end of World War II through the Korean War, depicted the impact of war upon individuals and the accompanying problem of social readjustment. The theme of afflicted veterans, like that of the cattle barons, centered on the alienation of individuals from the larger society. McComb's anger at having been ostracized by a country he had served in war is largely justified. Although carried to excessive lengths, McComb's determination to avenge his country's ingratitude must have struck a familiar and even

---

[10] Erich Fromm and Karen Horney are briefly discussed in Hartshorne, *Distorted Image,* p. 125. Fromm's views on man's psychological impulse for success and power and how this is frustrated in American society are discussed by John H. Schaar, *Escape from Authority: The Perspectives of Erich Fromm* (New York: Harper Torchbooks, 1961).

sympathetic chord with audiences who were anticipating the return of thousands of GIs into a peacetime economy. Although the GI Bill, together with an expanding economy, negated fears of veteran unrest such as had occurred after World War I, much of the argument on behalf of the bill reflected such fears.[11]

Since American soldiers had been directly exposed to extensive brutalities the reading public was learning about, it was logical to assume that many veterans had suffered emotional scars. Reinhold Niebuhr and other postwar writers expressed profound disillusionment over the extent of human beastliness as evidenced in particular by the Nazi atrocities. The war-crime revelations seemed to confirm Niebuhr's conclusions about the dark side of human nature that led him to question liberal assumptions of inevitable social progress.[12]

Westerns, likewise, depicted individual disillusionment and social discontent in the aftermath of the Civil War, as veterans returned to an uncertain future, cynical, confused, and hardened to the realities of violence. A favorite theme involved basically good men who are driven to lawless behavior by the trauma of war and its unsettling aftermath. As the old prospector tells Gregory Peck in *Yellow Sky* (1948), "the war" put a lot of young people on the wrong track.

Postwar Westerns about Jesse and Frank James attributed their lawlessness to the impact of the Civil War. In the 1939 version of *Jesse James*, the famous duo became outlaws to retaliate against the exploitation of poor folk, a familiar and identifiable situation for Depression-era Americans. After 1945 it was fashionable to blame the James's misconduct on the violence and confused values of wartime. In *Badman's Territory* (1946), one of several Westerns tailor-made for Randolph Scott by producer Nat Holt, the staunch law-and-order marshal (Scott) learns that the James brothers are actually good boys who re-

11 Debates surrounding passage of the GI Bill are analyzed by Keith Olson, *The G.I. Bill, the Veterans, and the Colleges* (Lexington: University Press of Kentucky, 1974), pp. 1–24.

12 Reinhold Niebuhr, *The Children of Light and the Children of Darkness: A Vindication of Democracy and a Critique of Its Traditional Defense* (New York: Charles Scribner's Sons, 1944), pp. 9–22. These pages appear in Eisinger, ed., *The 1940s*, pp. 432–39.

ceived a bad start with Quantrill's raiders. The outlaws prove
better people than certain greedy bounty hunters who proclaim
themselves lawmen. In *Kansas Raiders* (1951), Jesse (Audie
Murphy) rides with the demagogue Quantrill (Brian Donlevy)
during the Civil War to avenge the burning of his home by
Yankees. He rationalizes what he suspects is unjustifiable violence as an act of war in which killing and burning are condoned
as legal and even heroic. Walter Brennan, a former Quantrill
raider in *Best of the Bad Men* (1951), likewise muses about the
illogic of being hunted as an outlaw after the Civil War for
actions that are sanctioned in wartime.

    *Kansas Raiders* and *Best of the Bad Men* remain unique among
Westerns, because their alienated outlaw figures are neither killed
nor totally won over to the ways of social respectability. After
mistakenly participating in Quantrill's bloody raids, Jesse James
in *Kansas Raiders* eludes the law and rides off a free man. He is
wiser for having recognized the evil of his deeds; yet, when a
young compatriot bids him farewell with a comment about apply-
ing the banditry tactics learned from Quantrill, he replies, "That's
fine, Kip." The hero of *Best of the Bad Men* intends to turn himself in, but at the end of the film offers his best wishes to two of
his less scrupulous comrades, one of whom says he will prospect
for gold in California and the other that there is also gold a
lot closer, at the Denver mint. These films were not advocating
lawlessness and social irresponsibility, but they did convey mis-
givings about a legal order that is marred by war-related injustices
and turmoil.

    In most outlaw Westerns, such as *The Fabulous Texan* (1947),
*Three Godfathers* (1948), *Yellow Sky* (1948), *The Doolins of
Oklahoma* (1949), *Streets of Laredo* (1949), *Colorado Territory* (1949), *Branded* (1951), *The Great Missouri Raid* (1951
—another James gang variation), *Al Jennings of Oklahoma*
(1951), *Jack Slade* (1953), and *Jack McCall, Desperado*
(1953), the alienated individual either dies for his sins against
society or reforms. The same applies to women desperadoes, such
as Jane Russell's *Montana Belle* (1952) or Barbara Stanwyck's
*Maverick Queen* (1956).

    *Al Jennings of Oklahoma* typifies Westerns sympathetic to

war-alienated individuals who eventually reconcile themselves with a flawed but basically good society. Its opening sequence implies that the Civil War has caused the title character's lawlessness from the moment of his birth. A baby is heard crying while Union troops raid a southern home, and Al's brother remarks that Al already sounds mad about something. As the child of a war that marked the breakdown of peace and social order, Al Jennings carries into adulthood an impatience with legalities that so often seem incongruous with human injustice. By the end of the film, however, Al realizes that love and happiness require him to forsake outlawry and assume a responsible role in society. After five years in jail—his sentence commuted by Theodore Roosevelt—Al becomes a lawyer in the great Sooner commonwealth of Oklahoma.

Whether set in Oklahoma, Texas (*Dallas* [1950], *Lone Star* [1952]), Mexico (*Vera Cruz* [1954]), or Cuba (*Santiago* [1956]), Westerns affirmed the importance of the veteran's adjustment to meet the still greater challenges awaiting a state or nation. The disillusioned veteran must eventually overcome his personal injuries and join the cause of freedom and progress. The importance attributed to veterans' rehabilitation programs after World War II and the Korean War derived in large part from their function as a means by which the nation might utilize its manpower reserves to build a better tomorrow in a world still wracked by international rivalry.[13]

The central characters of *The Man from Colorado* (1948) and *Horizons West* (1951) were less fortunate in overcoming their war-induced emotional instability. Both films focus on men who are unable to adjust to peacetime because of what the Civil War did to them psychologically. In *Horizons West*, Dan Hammond (Robert Ryan), a hard-working Texas rancher before the

[13] Henry H. Kessler, in *Rehabilitation of the Physically Handicapped* (New York: Columbia University Press, 1953), pp. 234–35, writes that the large number of physically handicapped persons, including war casualties, "are a serious threat to the capacity of the nation to meet the demands of war. . . . We face new problems. We cannot wait to be aroused again by dynamic nations and seething populations emerging from the chaos of the war with increasing strength as they utilize the advances of modern machinery, organization, and transportation."

war, recognizes that the war has stretched his appetite for wealth and power, and he proceeds to grab what he can. When he breaks the law, he must confront his half-brother (Rock Hudson), who has emerged from the war unscathed to resume a quiet rural life. Although the brother remains the film's ideal of a socially responsible individual, all dramatic interest lies with Dan's tragically warped character.

Maniacal, killer impulses engendered by war gradually resurface in the character of Owen Devereaux (Glenn Ford), a Yankee hero appointed territorial judge in *The Man from Colorado*. In the first part of this film, Devereaux is more pathetic than evil, since he is frantically aware of the growing insanity that has nearly overcome him in the last days of the war. Pride and false hopes of recovery move him to feign normality, but he soon becomes paranoid at the slightest hint from anyone that he needs help. His close friend and comrade-in-arms, Del Stewart (William Holden), hides his suspicions of Devereaux's imbalance in the belief that any veteran deserves all the time and help in resuming a normal life that a community can afford. As the town marshal trying to prevent violence between a mining company and angry veterans whose lands and jobs have been displaced by the company, Stewart at one point chides the town citizenry for denying the veterans an even break after their years of sacrifice in war. It is with the greatest reluctance, therefore, that Stewart must eventually expose Devereaux's madness, which has led him to inflict a reign of terror on the community.

Man's irrationality, with or without the context of war, became a major preoccupation of Hollywood storytellers. Whether in the form of suspense thrillers (Alfred Hitchcock's *Shadow of a Doubt* [1942], *Spellbound* [1945], *Strangers on a Train* [1951]), topical melodramas (*Crossfire* [1947], *The Snake Pit* [1949]), or Westerns (*The Man from Colorado*), filmmakers during the forties reflected doubt about man as a progressive, rational creature in total control of his actions. Leading characters took on the qualities of Niebuhr's "children of darkness," fallible creatures susceptible to feelings and actions beyond their control. Similar assumptions colored the neo-conservative school of thought, which challenged liberal naïvete about man's innate

*The Man from Colorado* (Columbia, 1948). The psychological impact of war on the returning veteran.

goodness and rationality. Postwar commentators found wide-spread anxiety reflected in the growing numbers of mental patients and those seeking psychoanalysis and tranquilizers.[14]

Freudian overtones characterize Raoul Walsh's *Pursued* (1947), in which the hero (Robert Mitchum) is beset by seemingly unexplainable bizarre happenings. The only clue lies hidden in sporadic flashes of memory about a mysterious childhood occurrence—photographed in eerie dreamlike fashion by James Wong Howe. In *Duel in the Sun* (1946), Jennifer Jones stars as a hapless child of raw emotion and passion who struggles, with all best intentions, to become a lady; but she cannot rationally cope with the racist slurs on her Indian blood or the lascivious advances of her guardian's wild son (Gregory Peck).

The postwar emphasis on the psychologically perturbed western hero was most successfully developed by director Anthony Mann. The first of five Westerns directed by Mann with James Stewart as the hero, *Winchester 73* (1950), established both men as promising westerners of the fifties. In the Westerns Stewart made for Mann (*Winchester 73* [1950], *Bend of the River* [1952], *The Naked Spur* [1953], *The Far Country* [1955], and *The Man from Laramie* [1956]), he plays a lonely individual who is driven to extremes of physical and mental anguish as he hunts those responsible for some personal or family tragedy. In the process he is usually separated from the community to which he must ultimately return if he is to know any meaningful happiness and fulfillment. The community is pictured as progressive, a source of individual stability and sanity, in contrast with the harsh and violent wilderness where loneliness, physical hardship, and raw emotion nearly overcome the hero.

*Winchester 73* begins in a settled town where law and order prevail, whereas the remainder of the story subjects Stewart to a hostile environment of marauding Indians and vicious outlaws. By the time he catches up with his patricidal brother, Stewart is consumed with rage at the evil he must eradicate for his own peace of mind. In *The Naked Spur*, the hero's psychological anguish and self-destructive obsession with violent reprisal becomes

14 William E. Leuchtenburg, *A Troubled Feast: American Society since 1945* (Boston: Little, Brown, 1973), p. 104.

most explicit. Ever since his wife had left him and sold his ranch while he was away at war, Howard Kemp (Stewart) has been a ruthless bounty hunter, killing for money. His coarse amorality and materialism reflect disillusionment with a deceitful world. And again it is the war that proves the detrimental turning point in the hero's heretofore peaceful life. Anxiety arises, however, because Kemp can never totally submerge his basic humanity and yearning for the old way of life. In a moment of weakness, he reminisces to the heroine (Janet Leigh) about the joys of his former life: "I had neighbors, you know . . . the Websters had four sons, each skinnier than the other; always comin' over to lend a hand; didn't give you much chance to get lonesome. The house—the house ain't much, but it's just prime cattle country. The fella that owns the ranch now, he's willin' to sell." Only after considerable physical violence and mental anguish bordering on insanity does Kemp accept the heroine's offer of a new start in life.

The emotional and physical self-destructiveness of being up-rooted from the community also characterizes Fritz Lang's *Rancho Notorious* (1952). In this film the embittered, vengeful Vern Haskell (Arthur Kennedy) cannot rest until he has found the rapist-killer of his wife. His life as a peaceful family man has been destroyed, and he is doomed to a lonely and violent life. His search takes him away from the good society to an outlaw stronghold, where he mixes company with other ill-fated outcasts. The film ends as Vern rides off with a gunman acquaintance, while an off-screen voice sings: "Two men rode away from Chuckaluck and death rode beside them on the trail, for they died that day, so the legends tell, with empty guns they fought and fell. So ends the tale of hate, murder, and revenge."

In Lang's film, as well as those of Mann, fate deals the hero a nasty blow, although with Lang less depends on the hero's struggle to resolve his own psychological malaise. Lang's heroes (in *The Big Heat* and *Moonfleet,* as well as *Rancho Notorious*) are fallible creatures but more completely trapped in a cosmos of predetermined corruption and destruction than are Mann's, who could achieve salvation. Lang also conveys less faith in the community as a source of human justice and dignity. In one sequence from *Rancho Notorious,* the hero is tossed in jail for unwittingly trying to buy liquor on election day. The town, evidently up in arms against the present officeholders, is using the liquor issue to oust them. It matters little that the hero is an innocent bystander.

An indication of the prominence of the alienated hero theme is the casting of major western stars after 1945 as psychologically troubled or as social outcasts. John Wayne, who even as an outlaw in *Stagecoach* had been self-assured, in *The Angel and the Badman* (1946) plays a gunman torn between his rough-and-ready, violent life and the pacifist philosophy of the Quaker girl he loves. In *Red River* (1948), as a cattleman desperate to drive his cattle to market to save himself and Texas economically, Wayne becomes an obsessed tyrant who is oblivious of the welfare and rights of other men. In *The Searchers* (1956), John Ford drew Wayne's best and most complex performance, as an aging frontiersman blinded by racist hatred for the Comanches who massacred his family. As an outlaw in *Four Faces West* (1948) and *Colorado Territory* (1949), Joel McCrea struggles to cope with a world that seems to oppose him at every turn. In *Ramrod* he suffers guilt from having lost his wife in a fire while he was away from the ranch. Even the ordinarily stalwart Randolph Scott could not escape guilt at having contributed to one of Quantrill's terrifying raids in *The Stranger Wore a Gun* (1953), and he becomes irrationally vengeful in *Tall Man Riding* (1955) and Budd Boetticher's *Decision at Sundown*. In most of Boetticher's Westerns, Scott is doomed to loneliness, forever deprived of the settled home life he had once known. His last role, in *Ride the High Country* (1962), was that of a disillusioned ex-marshal who resorts to thievery to attain the wealth and status that have always been denied him as a lawman. Alan Ladd, the ultimate laconic mythic hero in *Shane* (1953), turns insane killer in *One Foot in Hell* (1960) to avenge his wife's death.

Particularly adept in roles as guilt-ridden or neurotic Westerners during the fifties are actors Glenn Ford and Kirk Douglas. Ford, in *Jubal* (1956), plays a rejected bastard who is hated by his mother for not having drowned instead of his father. In *The Fastest Gun Alive* (1956), he cannot escape the memory of having been too cowardly to shoot the man who killed his father. Douglas, similarly, in *Along the Great Divide* (1951), blames himself for not having averted his father's death. In *Gunfight at the O.K. Corral* (1957), he stresses neurotic elements in the character of Doc Holliday that Cesar Romero and Victor Mature had barely suggested in earlier versions. As the *Man without a Star* (1955), he is forever wandering, because he cannot accept a civilization of fenced ranges that reminds him of a horrible maiming with barbed wire.

Gregory Peck emerged as the supreme alienated western hero with *Yellow Sky* (1948) and, especially, *The Gunfighter* (1950) and *The Bravados* (1958). As *The Gunfighter,* Peck memorably portrays the tragic Jimmy Ringo, whose reputation with a gun makes him the target of every fast gun in the West, a man no decent community can tolerate. Although this film was not a box office hit, one film writer found in it "a metaphor . . . pertinent to the mood of the year in which it was first shown." In it Ringo, a tired man, was seeking peace, even as the audience was seeking solace after the tensions of World War II.[15] The same metaphor would seem to apply in general to many Westerns where the hero—especially in the aftermath of the Civil War—is denied respite in perpetually troubled times.

Toward the end of *The Gunfighter,* Ringo sardonically observes that he is thirty-five years old and does not even own a watch. He is disillusioned with a lifestyle that once offered adventure and escape but instead produced fear, self-disgust, and waste. He then sets out to win back his wife and young son, to start a new life; but his wife is reluctant to sacrifice the security of her life as a schoolteacher for a man who had once left her. She fails to understand that Ringo truly wants a quiet, respectable life and that society denies him that life by rejecting him and encouraging the violence he deplores. The townspeople seem intolerably righteous in their aspersions against him; children gawk in admiration of his fast gun; and menfolk stand around as though reluctant to miss any excitement that a gunfight might bring to their dull lives. The saloon owner (Karl Malden) treats Ringo

15 Gow, *Hollywood in the Fifties,* p. 67.

*The Gunfighter* (Twentieth Century Fox, 1950). The alienated hero: a target for every fast gun in the West; a man no "decent" society can tolerate.

with condescending politeness, knowing that the gunfighter's fame will bring in a good business from curiosity seekers. The only person who can empathize with Ringo is the sheriff because he too had once been an outlaw; but he had reformed before it was too late. Yet, in spite of his empathy, the sheriff's responsibility to the town's safety obliges him to send Ringo on his way. As Ringo leaves town, after having extracted from his wife a promise to consider a new life with him, he is shot down by a young gun who wants to be number one. The sheriff tells the assailant that all he has won is the kind of life Ringo was trying to escape. The town mourns Ringo's death and gives him a church funeral, and his wife reveals that she is Mrs. Ringo.

Not since *The Ox Bow Incident* had a Western taken such a critical viewpoint toward the frontier townspeople for other than racial prejudice. In this respect *The Gunfighter* foreshadowed the many Westerns, especially after 1952, that took a jaundiced view of the quality and standards of the very civilization western heroes were supposed to defend and promote. Self-centered individualism without social affiliation meant loneliness and unhappiness for the individual, and only through adjustment to the greater society could the individual find salvation. Yet *The Gunfighter* also criticized the community for harboring a vicarious thirst for violence while condemning the man of violence and encouraging the kind of role-playing exhibited by Ringo's wife. It is, in fact, difficult to imagine Ringo ever having lived in such a place without compromising or falsifying his identity. For all of the loneliness, violence, and self-disgust that characterized Ringo's wasted life, he had at least acquired a dignity and integrity that distinguished him from the common citizenry. The final scene of *The Gunfighter* is, significantly, neither an idyllic small town nor an image of a proud, bustling nation, but rather a transparent, ghostly Ringo riding the skies.

The enormous influence of *The Gunfighter* can be seen in numerous repetitions and variations on the same theme in western movies throughout the fifties. Television producers based several Western series, such as *The Restless Gun* and *Gunslinger,* on the lonely, reformed gunfighter motif. *The Gunfighter* was remade for television in 1955 as *End of a Gun,* with Richard Conte playing the role of Jimmy Ringo. Moreover, many of the fifties' gunfighter Westerns would continue to combine concern for the individual's alienation with society's failure to cope with that alienation. Doubts about the value of the American community as conveyed by Westerns like *The Ox Bow Incident, The Gunfighter,* and *Rancho Notorious* would receive greater attention in the future. With a relaxation of the Production Code and the demise of McCarthyism in Hollywood after 1953, Westerns, like other films, reflected greater liberty in addressing America's weaknesses as well as its strengths.

CHAPTER SIX

# SOCIETY IN THE 1950S: COMPLACENT OR PLAINTIVE?

P
OPULAR CULTURE, CERTAINLY
including movies, came under the fire of social critics during
the fifties as a prime reflection and cause of an appalling complacency and conformism that afflicted modern America.[1] Most
Westerns before, and many during, the fifties seem to verify this
indictment, in that they resolve problems of social danger and
personal alienation through final social commitment. Gunfighters
and other loners continued through the fifties to correct their
irresponsible behavior or mangled psyches through civic duty
and social allegiance.

Perpetual alienation, as in Kirk Douglas's troubled nonconformists in *Gunfight at the O.K. Corral* (1956) and *Man without
a Star* (1955) or John Wayne's obsessive Indian hater in *The
Searchers* (1956), was viewed with considerable sadness, given
the film's identification of personal happiness with communal
affiliation. Yet, beginning with *The Gunfighter* (1950) and to a
larger extent in the Westerns after 1953, the problem of personal
reconcilation with society related directly to, or accompanied
failings within, the society itself. If the hero needed redeeming,
so also did the community toward which he must aspire.

Westerns increasingly questioned the quality of community
life in terms similar to contemporary social criticisms of postwar
America's placid and conformist character. The assumption of
fifties intellectuals that the mass of society was contented and
conforming has generally been accepted as valid, especially as
compared with the outbursts of political and social consciousness

[1] See, for example, MacDonald, *Against the American Grain*, pp. 3–75.

in the following decade. The prevalence of such themes in fifties Westerns makes clear, however, that self-criticism characterized popular as well as intellectual thought. If one judges from the Westerns produced for a mass audience, the decade of the 1950s appears less complacent than complaining in its popular views.

Fifties intellectuals focused their criticism on the debilitating implications of a homogeneous consumer society. Labels such as "The Packaged Society," "Lonely Crowd," and "Organization Man" signified dissatisfaction with society's passive acceptance of a standardized, affluent lifestyle. Antiseptic suburbs, where families kept up with the Joneses in their standardized houses; the uninspired "silent generation" of college students, content with nothing more than achieving a secure corporate career; the simplistic homilies of Billy Graham or Norman Vincent Peale on togetherness or positive thinking; and the manipulation of consumers by Madison Avenue were commonly attacked as symptoms of social malaise at a time when international tensions and domestic crises (especially the racial problem) demanded an immediate and strong national response.[2]

At the political level, both conservative and liberal critics identified Eisenhower's middle-of-the-road Republicanism and lack of decisive leadership with the larger weaknesses of a society that had lost its sense of direction and creative spirit. None of these critics implied the need for a radical overhaul of the socio-political system, as many sixties critics would advocate; and, in fact, many historians of the fifties pointed to the blessings of a national consensus. Traditional American ideals and the system of government worked out by the nation's enlightened fore-fathers were adequate to meet present-day challenges, if only Americans would recall and live up to the national heritage.[3] Whether a conservative bemoaned liberal deviance from the con-stitutional framework of limited government or a liberal faulted Eisenhower with inaction and drift, political criticism, like the

---

[2] Leuchtenburg, *A Troubled Feast,* pp. 69–80, provides a brief but useful summary of intellectual criticisms.

[3] A major statement of the consensus view of American history is Daniel Boorstin, *The Genius of American Politics* (Chicago: University of Chicago Press, 1953).

intellectual-social criticism of rampant conformity and individual anxiety, connoted dissatisfaction with an America that had lost all sense of direction and purpose. America, it was believed, could ill afford such weaknesses at a time when the rest of the world either challenged or depended upon U.S. leadership.

That this troubled state of mind about America was not merely the property of intellectuals suffering status anxieties or politicians contending for the next election is suggested by the motion picture's preoccupation with many of the same concerns. No better illustration of this exists than the socially critical direction taken by the Westerns of this decade. The first and most obvious example of the Western's more critical view of society appears in the racial commentaries of *Broken Arrow* and successive revisions of the Indian theme. The reconcilation of hero and community in these Westerns depended less upon the hero's social adjustment than upon the redemption of a bigoted society. By the mid-fifties, a few Westerns, such as *The Broken Lance* (1954), *The Last Frontier* (1956), and *Reprisal* (1956), suggest that bigotry is not an isolated failing or the product of a few warped minds, but is fed and perpetuated by the placid and conformist character of the larger society. These films juxtapose individual conscience and honesty with social role-playing, hypocrisy, and opportunism. Racism, therefore, becomes sympomatic of a deeper and more pervasive inadequacy. In this respect, these Westerns about the Indian share many of the reservations concerning American society that were so notably emphasized by *High Noon* (1952).

The most significant turning point in the Western's treatment of the individual-societal relationship, *High Noon* reversed the current motif of alienated hero seeking redemption through commitment to the good society. In this film a stalwart marshal steadfastly executes his duty according to the dictates of conscience, in spite of conformist pressures and the reprimands of an uncommitted citizenry. Film critic Pauline Kael called *High Noon* a "primer sociology" and a "microcosm of the evils of capitalist society."[4] The film does resemble contemporary social criticisms

---

[4] Pauline Kael, *Kiss Kiss Bang Bang* (New York: Bantam Books, 1969), pp. 185, 349.

*High Noon* (United Artists, 1952). A townspeople's amiability hides civic cowardice and self-interest.

by the intellectual world regarding conformity, complacency, and obsession with material security. Leading citizens of the town, including the judge, the parson, the marshal's predecessor, and the town councilmen, encourage Marshal Kane to leave town rather than risk a violent encounter with villains who have sworn to kill him. A councilman argues that his presence may erupt into the kind of violence that would endanger investors' confidence in a town with an enviable image of peace and security. Kane's predecessor and the judge urge him to leave, because they believe the town's ultimate complacency mocks the preservation of law and human rights. The judge sees the town as analogous to the decay in civic consciousness that befell ancient Athens.

Aside from the complacency and fear that grip most of the town's citizens, the film alludes to those who want Kane out of the way, because his strict law enforcement has discouraged the big spenders who prefer a wide-open town. Selfish opportunism emerges most clearly in the person of Kane's deputy Harvey (Lloyd Bridges), who hates Kane for not having recommended him as his successor. Harvey covets the status that Kane held in the community as well as the attentions of Kane's former mistress, Helen Ramirez (Katy Jurado). With the character of Helen Ramirez and the town's resentment toward her, the film added racism and snobbery to its list of indictments.

This unusually critical view of an outwardly respectable community did not escape notice in Hollywood where John Wayne objected to the film's being anti-American. How else was one to interpret "Ole Coop putting the United States marshal's badge under his foot and stepping on it?" One local newspaper observed that emphasis on the town's weakness makes *High Noon* the kind of film that elicits cries of communist propaganda and that the undue stress on human frailty draws suspicion, "with some justification, considering the international crisis."[5]

Carl Foreman claims to have written *High Noon* as an allegory of the fear that had gripped the Hollywood community in the face of anticommunist investigations by the House Un-American Activities Committee (HUAC). He even used the fictional town name of "Hadleyville" to suggest Hollywood. Foreman

[5] *Playboy*, May 1971, p. 90; *Citizen News*, August 19, 1952, p. 13.

wrote his screenplay while under subpoena by HUAC to testify about his alleged communist affiliation. He admittedly fashioned Marshal Kane's predicament of choosing between conscience and conformity to community pressures as analogous with his own situation of being prodded to collaborate with those he knew to be violating civil liberties. Hadleyville's surrender of civic responsibility in tolerating the four gunmen was in his mind comparable to Hollywood's collaboration with the congressional investigation.[6]

In its issue of January 10, 1953, the *Nation* praised New York critics for selecting *High Noon* as best picture of the year, especially in view of Foreman's having been black-listed in Hollywood for refusing to testify before HUAC. The *Nation* concluded: "There must be times these days when Mr. Foreman feels that he too [like Marshal Kane in *High Noon*] has been deserted by those who should have helped him stand off the bullies and tough guys whose aggressions have so largely destroyed the moral fiber of the Western town that goes by the name of Hollywood."

Loved by liberal critics in the East and damned by conservatives in Hollywood, Foreman's alleged polemic seems to have filtered through this classic Western. Yet the manner in which Foreman structured his analogy bears an unmistakable similarity to the anticommunist arguments of those he was attacking. Could not Joseph McCarthy himself be identified with the strong individualist who refuses to compromise with that which threatens the community? Kane, of course, was defending himself; but he knew that the gunmen, if unopposed, could ride roughshod over the town. Moreover, Kane's unpopularity for choosing to fight rather than abide with Hadleyville's do-nothing policy is akin to McCarthy's self-image of a crusader risking "smear and abuse" from those upset by his forthright approach.

That Foreman's liberal polemic should so resemble the arguments and approach of those whom he attacked is indicative of the common assumptions shared by both pro- and anti-McCarthy forces. Each sought in its own fashion to define America's ap-

[6] Arthur C. Knight, interview with Carl Foreman, January 2, 1964, Special Collections, Doheny Library, University of Southern California, Los Angeles.

parent malaise in coping with domestic and international exigencies in terms of some concrete evil within society itself. McCarthy pictured liberal appeasers and their duped public supporters as selling out the nation, whereas his liberal opponents saw McCarthyism as fostering a terrifying conformity that threatened the freedoms by which America must stand in opposition to its totalitarian antithesis abroad. No one could argue with the basic premise of *High Noon* that society cannot afford civic complacency when threatened by destructive forces. Blind conformity to a misguided course of action (or inaction) would endanger the thoughtful unanimity that was considered essential for America's survival. Margaret Chase Smith stressed the point in her famous senatorial speech against McCarthy in 1950: "As an American, I am shocked at the way Republicans and Democrats alike are playing directly into the Communist design of 'confuse, divide, and conquer'."[7]

With the success of *High Noon* and especially the decline of McCarthyism by 1954 as a major influence on Hollywood's depiction of America, Westerns became increasingly critical of the settled frontier community. Like Hadleyville, the fictional towns bore all the characteristics of conformism, material selfishness, and complacency that modern political and social critics attributed to the affluent middle-class society of the fifties. Westerns explored both the social implications of endangered individualism (e.g., identity problems, false values, role-playing) and the political-diplomatic problem of society's being able to withstand internal corruption and external challenges.

Following the precedent of *High Noon,* Westerns commonly discussed social failings in terms of the citizenry's dereliction of civic responsibility against some external threat. Once the struggle to establish civilization in a raw frontier had been accomplished, the settled townspeople began to lose the energy and courage needed to preserve their freedom. *Shane* (1953) and other Westerns continued the more traditional format of the heroic gunman saving the day for the decent but dependent settlers and thus redeeming himself—if necessary—through commit-

[7] Thomas A. Bailey, ed., *The American Spirit: United States History as Seen by Contemporaries* (Boston: D. C. Heath, 1963), p. 896.

ment to the good society. What *High Noon* and growing numbers of other Westerns suggested, however, is that the society itself needs redeeming. Without collective determination to resist evil elements, there was little any individual could do. Alienated heroes still needed social reconciliation as in Westerns of the late forties, but there was an added element of doubt as to whether society's weakness made such a reconciliation worthwhile.

Two of Randolph Scott's Westerns, *A Lawless Street* (1955) and *Decision at Sundown* (1957), suggest that the hero's agonizing confrontation with the town's villains might have been avoided had the townspeople not turned their backs on lawlessness to begin with. As the town sheriff in *A Lawless Street*, Scott faces Marshal Kane's predicament in *High Noon* of defending the law without support of the citizenry. In a scene where Scott pretends to be dead and the streets are overrun with gun-happy riffraff, director Joseph H. Lewis has conjured up a terrifying vision of anarchy. In this case the hero can save society not by protecting it but by constructing a situation in which it will prove its own need to be responsible. Then, when Scott returns to the much relieved citizenry, they help him clean up the town. He can happily remove his badge and tell the people they no longer need him, since they now possess the means and determination to look after themselves. In *Decision at Sundown* Scott finds it more difficult to forgive the townspeople, whose dereliction of civic responsibility has brought him personal tragedy; but he can leave the town knowing that they at least have become aware of the consequences of their inaction.

Films like *Top Gun* (1955), *Man Alone* (1955), *Tension at Table Rock* (1956), and *The Tin Star* (1957) combine the theme of the ostracized gunman of *The Gunfighter* (1950) with the socially critical law-and-order context of *High Noon*. Whereas the townspeople in these films exclude the disreputable gunman from their ranks, he represents a kind of honesty and dignity necessary to eradicate the dangers to which society has closed its eyes. The hero's eventual commitment to a socially respectable life is accompanied by society's commitment to begin practicing the civic virtues it had merely preached.

In *The Tin Star*, director Anthony Mann continues the theme of his Westerns with James Stewart, in which an alienated hero finds happiness through social commitment, but in this case Mann is less confident about the worth of society. Dudley Nichols, who wrote the screenplay, had formerly expressed reservations about the artificial values of frontier civilization in *Stagecoach* (1939). In *The Tin Star,* Nichols and Mann emphasize the racism, hypocrisy, and pettiness of the townspeople, while dramatizing an alienated bounty hunter's (Henry Fonda) acceptance of social responsibility.

The bounty hunter had once quit his job as an official law enforcer because the public was using him to do their dirty work without offering him support. He learns, however, that if he does not take back "the tin star" to help a young and inexperienced sheriff (Anthony Perkins) the town may have no law at all. After the hero's eventual assistance in defeating the bad guy, the townspeople appear grateful; but there is little suggestion (as in former Westerns of this type) of a positive, active role to be played by the ordinary citizen or of any social change brought about by his action. Law and order depends primarily on the power and professionalism of the honest, committed lawman, without whom a generally fickle and weak-willed populace would be open prey.

Thus, *The Tin Star* lacks the indignant tone of *High Noon*'s stab at society. Whereas the latter film concludes with a disgusted Marshal Kane throwing away his badge out of disgust with an unworthy society, the former has its hero fatalistically accepting society's weaknesses and recommitting himself with no illusions about those whom he is sworn to protect. The hero shoulders the burden of society's welfare; but, unlike the classical Western, he does so with no sense of the intrinsic worth of the society he chooses to guard. Society will not change, so personal fulfillment comes solely from doing one's job rather than from promoting communal progress.

A more obvious exception to those fifties Westerns since *High Noon* that held society accountable for not responding collectively in defense of law and order is Paramount's *Gunfight at the O.K. Corral* (1957). Released the same year as Paramount's *The Tin Star, Gunfight* was produced on a much more lavish

*The Tin Star* (Paramount, 1957). Middle-class scorn for the lawman turned bounty hunter.

scale. This production had the classic look of an old-fashioned, epic encounter between good guy and bad guy, without the socially conscious motif of *High Noon* or *The Tin Star*. Yet this version of Wyatt Earp's encounters leading up to the famed shootout in Tombstone, Arizona, lacks the progressive social context of the traditional Western. The Earp-Clanton showdown becomes essentially a family affair of honor, without the motif of civilization battling savagery in the earlier John Ford version.

Ford's *My Darling Clementine* (1946) clearly identified Earp's campaign against lawlessness with the broader scheme of pioneers establishing order and decency in a new, untamed land. While Earp does have a family score to settle with the Clantons, his actions are continually interwoven with scenes of a thriving new community so as to unequivocally identify the hero with social progress.

By comparison, community life in *Gunfight at the O.K. Corral* serves only as a backdrop for the protagonists. Moreover, Earp's rescue of Doc Holliday from an angry lynch mob early in the film and his encounters with two crooked sheriffs (one of whom admits taking bribes because honesty merits only a low wage or death) suggest some of the undesirable aspects of society that were receiving heightened emphasis in other Westerns of the fifties.

Another feature Western, *Rio Bravo* (1959), stood conspicuously apart from the trend of social criticism but nevertheless reflected a departure from the traditional emulation of a progressive society. Director Howard Hawks deliberately set out to contest what he considered to be a ridiculous notion in *High Noon*: the marshal's expectation of help from the citizenry to combat lawlessness. Hawks's sheriff in *Rio Bravo*, John T. Chance (played by John Wayne, whose patriotic sensibilities had been offended by *High Noon*), never asks for public assistance and even refuses it when offered, because he knows that amateurs just get in the way of a job that should be handled by professionals. Only Chance and his handpicked deputies can successfully defend the jailhouse against Nathan Burdette's cutthroats.

Again, as in *Gunfight at the O.K. Corral, Rio Bravo* confines its dramatic action to personal conflicts and interactions among the leading characters and avoids implications concerning the strength and progress of society. At stake is not the success or failure of society but the honor and self-esteem of the few major characters. The brief glimpses of town life allowed by director Hawks suggest a quiet mediocrity hardly deserving of the deadly battle for control of the jailhouse, especially when compared with the epic march of society Hawks used as backdrop to *Red River* (1948). As Robin Wood has pointed out in his analysis of Hawks's films, in *Rio Bravo* Hawks emphasized man's responsibility to himself rather than to society.[8]

Whereas *Gunfight at the O.K. Corral* and *Rio Bravo* represent the best that late-fifties Westerns could say about the strength of American society by nearly removing the social context altogether, *Man with the Gun* (1955) and *Warlock* (1959) probe the depths to which a weak citizenry could fall. In each of the latter films, a town has lost all semblance of law and order and must resort in desperation to hiring mercenaries to clean up the mess. Although some citizens recognize that their hired gunmen may prove as dangerous as the villains they defeat, they fear even more the risk of losing home and family if they should personally oppose the lawless elements that dominate the town. The hero mercenary in each film stands superior to the banal and selfish citizenry. As he efficiently dispatches lawless elements, he confronts the righteous townspeople, who are resentful of his power over them and who reprove his violent ways. The citizenry need his violent skills, but they simultaneously reject his character as being antithetical to their own notion of respectability.

What distinguishes the mercenary from his clientele is what divides the gunfighter or marshal from the populace, namely character, dignity, and forthrightness. In a given emergency the hero operates with what David Riesman termed "inner-directedness," an internalized sense of right and wrong divorced from the weak and shifting values of his social surrounding. The townspeople, on the other hand, forever compromise on a particular challenge, with little concern for anything but personal safety and material status. When the hero mercenary in *Man with the*

---

[8] Robin Wood, *Howard Hawks* (Garden City, N.Y.: Doubleday, 1968), pp. 49–50.

*Gun* (Robert Mitchum) angrily burns down a saloon that has been a gathering place for the lawless, the owner complains about having lost all that good lumber. Decency, respectability, and the like become righteous euphemisms that disguise a lack of meaningful values.

Most of these Westerns, whether they involve hired town tamers, reformed gunfighters, or lawmen, relate to what both conservative and liberal critics consider to be a weakening of the social fabric, reinforced by a lack of decisive leadership in America, that endangers the nation's power and responsibility in the world.[9]

Given the context of a weak society in Westerns of the fifties, it is not surprising that several films emphasized the danger of the unprincipled demagogue. Although the vision of a spineless society could appeal to either left or right, the prospect of a false prophet misleading a blind society seems most appropriate as an allegorical attack on McCarthyism.

*Johnny Guitar* (1954), *A Man Alone* (1955), and *Bad Day at Black Rock* (1955) each focused on individuals who fall victim to communities that are dominated by self-appointed pillars of respectability. The nonconforming social outcasts of Nicholas Ray's *Johnny Guitar* are nearly hanged by the so-called respectable citizens who are sheepishly manipulated by a ruthless cattle baron and a neurotic spinster. Together the two whip up public rage to exterminate a strong-willed heroine, whose independent ways threaten the status quo. In its fetid atmosphere and its con-

---

[9] Joseph McCarthy, Estes Kefauver, and John McClellan raised the spectre of corruption in America, while conservatives criticized the Warren court's extension of civil liberties as endangering national security and violating majority rights. Liberals like Adlai Stevenson assailed Republican leadership during the fifties as fostering "private opulence and public squalor." Leuchtenburg, *A Troubled Feast*, p. 110. Walter Lippmann wrote about the lack of informed, decisive leadership that afflicted this democracy, where public opinion interfered with policy-making. Walter Lippmann, *The Public Philosophy* (New York: Mentor Book, 1955). The launching of Sputnik I by the Soviets drew from Democrats criticism of Eisenhower's failure to keep ahead of the Russians. Even the prominent Republican voice of Claire Booth Luce was heard to say that the sound of the Russian Sputniks was an "outer-space raspberry to a decade of American pretensions that the American way of life is a gilt-edge guarantee of our national superiority." Goldman, *Crucial Decade*, p. 315.

viction that conventional people are really sick and bent on destroying outsiders who are at least comparatively wholesome, *Johnny Guitar* prefigured some motifs of the 1960s. Now, however, the hero was no longer expected to overcome his psychosis and conform but rather to fight for his life against the personal and social hysteria of the rest of society.

*A Man Alone* similarly contrasts the integrity and courage of its alienated protagonist (Ray Milland) with the civic irresponsibility and hypocrisy of the respectable townspeople. The first half of the film involves the hero (a lonely gunfighter) and heroine psychoanalyzing each other so that each will face up to the things that trouble them. After having been restored to human wholeness through this small-group therapy, the two must contend with the corruption and public complacency in the town where the hero is hiding out. A town boss who pretends to be a respectable citizen inflames public sentiment against the hero for a crime that he himself has engineered.

Furthermore, the heroine learns that her father, the sheriff, is on the take from the town boss. She confronts him with his dishonesty after suffering his indignation about her relations with the gunfighter. He defensively explains that he was only looking after their interests. He and her mother, he says, had come west to start a new life; but, instead of a land of promise, they had found a dog-eat-dog life. After they had lost their ranch and her mother had worked herself to a premature death doing laundry, he had felt compelled to use any means to assure his daughter a safe and secure life. What divides father and daughter in this confrontation is the kind of generation gap that existed between the fifties' children of affluence and their parents, whose preoccupation with providing material security stemmed from having survived the Depression of the 1930s.

The sheriff eventually realizes the folly of his opportunism and proceeds to help the hero expose the town boss. The film concludes with the hero chastising citizens for allowing their town to rot. Yet he decides to settle (with the sheriff's daughter) in this town, because its shame may bring improvement and because the next town may be just as bad.

*Bad Day at Black Rock* used a contemporary setting to make

*A Man Alone* (Republic, 1955). The generation gap between a corruptly affluent sheriff and his daughter.

the same point about a western town allowing itself to be cowed by devious types. Spencer Tracy plays a veteran of World War II who arrives at an isolated desert town to deliver a medal to the father of a Japanese-American war hero. There he discovers that a racist rancher and his cronies had murdered the father during the war and that the townspeople have sheepishly collaborated in covering up the crime. They initially refuse to become involved in the veteran hero's investigation because, as one explains, they have to live here and cannot afford to upset people. Until guilt overcomes their reluctance to help the hero, these are the people that social and intellectual critics of the 1950s saw as populating the United States, men without individual character and integrity, made fearful by the desperate need to "get along" within their community.

Society's dehumanizing and oppressive impact on individuals often appeared as inherent in the values and quality of civilized life rather than as the work of some corrupt or demagogic type. Alfred Werker, a prolific but little-known director of minor Hollywood films, directed four Westerns (*The Last Posse* [1953], *Devil's Canyon* [1953], *Three Hours to Kill* [1954], and *At Gunpoint* [1955]) in which individuals suffer the injustice that results from society's mistaken notions about its own progress and respectability.

In *The Last Posse,* a town spokesman commemorates Founder's Day with a speech about how proud everyone deserves to be of their law and order, schools, churches, and especially "of our respectability." Yet, as the speaker's own actions later demonstrate, the rhetoric hardly reflects reality. Even as the citizens celebrate, a small rancher is preparing to rob a cattle baron who has financially ruined him and others like him with the community's tacit approval and legal sanction. During the course of a prolonged manhunt, the deputized citizens betray their own greed when they find the stolen money.

A righteous community in *Devil's Canyon* convicts an honest rancher of manslaughter, for shooting two scoundrels in self-defense. Public indigation at the rancher's having violated a law that strictly prohibits shooting in the streets overrides any consideration of his having had to defend himself. Sentenced to ten

*At Gunpoint* (Allied Artists, 1955). A storekeeper and his family ostracized for not conforming to a town's expectations.

years in the Yuma prison, the rancher bitterly questions the meaning of social progress. The same society that abhors violence in the streets supports an inhumane prison system that brutalizes and destroys the inmates.

An embittered gunman (Dana Andrews) returns home in *Three Hours to Kill* to avenge an attempted lynching that has left an ugly scar on his neck. Once an aspiring rancher and citizen, he had nearly been hanged by drunken "friends," who had mistakenly believed he had killed a man. After a narrow escape from hanging, Guthrie became a roving gunfighter, awaiting the day when he could get back at his would-be executioners and find the real murderer. Upon his return, guilty citizens greet him with considerable fear and discomfort. A saloon girl who loved Guthrie expresses genuine concern for the self-destructiveness of Guthrie's hate. "You've changed," she says. "They've [the towns-people] killed the Jim I knew." He replies: "That's right, they did." Only one other person shows Guthrie any sympathy, and he turns out to be the real killer. Justice is done and the towns-people ask Guthrie to stay, but he refuses and rides away knowing that he could never forget what they did to him. Knowledge of what the town is really like has killed both his desire to belong and his willingness to overlook moral evil.

Whereas the conclusion of Werker's *Three Hours to Kill* resembles that of *High Noon,* his next Western, *At Gunpoint,* seems almost a remake of that classic film. The unique feature of *At Gunpoint* is its focus on such a nontraditional western hero as the town storekeeper. Like most of the citizens of Plainview, storekeeper Jack Wright (Fred MacMurray) enjoys a comfortable middle-class life with his wife, boy, and dog. Then one day he inadvertently shoots a bank robber and brings upon himself the threat of reprisal by other members of the gang. At first the townspeople idolize Wright as their saving hero, but they desert him just as quickly when they realize that he really cannot shoot. In the hope of discouraging the gang from taking its wrath out on all of them, the town leaders urge Wright to leave; and, when he refuses, they proceed to snub him and boycott his store. The film ends with the community supporting Wright against the outlaws and apologizing for its callousness. But the sincerity of all the handshaking seems subject to question as the wise doctor, Wright's only supporter throughout the ordeal, goes off shaking his head.

Except for a momentary lapse into self-pity, for which Doc chides him (just as the saloon girl of *Three Hours to Kill* had warned Jim Guthrie about his self-consuming hate), Jack Wright, like *High Noon*'s Marshal Kane, remains generally stolid and self-assured in comparison with his unreliable, weak-willed neighbors. His strength of character emerges first and foremost when he withstands social pressures against doing what he knows to be right. Also, as in *High Noon,* the conflict between hero and society supersede in importance the violent encounter between hero and badmen. Yet, in creating a nonviolent, commoner hero, director Werker has made the test of heroism solely a matter of character, as opposed to Marshal Kane (and most western heroes) whose courage is inseparable from expertise with a six-gun. Werker in fact democratized the possibility of heroism in a cowardly society.

The story also deals with another theme central to the intellectual critique of the 1950s: that people are more concerned with image than with substance or real value. Such writers as David Riesman, William H. Whyte, Jr., C. Wright Mills, and Vance Packard perceived the modern tendency toward role-playing or the creation of a proper image for the sake of job and social advancement. Jack Wright's unusual integrity is proved not only by his refusal to flee but by his rejection of the role that society tries to pin on him. When he is hailed as the town savior, Wright both knows his limitations and can live comfortably with them; he thus avoids the temptation to act like the top gun everyone assumes him to be. He is too honest a man to engage in the kind of role-playing that so concerned social critics of the 1950s.

Other undistinguished, nonviolent types (like Jack Wright but lacking his fortitude to withstand conformist pressures or to cope with society's erroneous notions of what is meant to be "a man") appear in *The Fastest Gun Alive* (1956) and *Johnny Concho* (1956). In *The Fastest Gun Alive,* George Temple (Glenn Ford), who also is a storekeeper and family man, suffers from feelings of inadequacy in a society that identifies manliness with gun skill. His inferiority complex is reinforced by guilt concerning a cowardly act that caused the death of his father. To gain the respect and manly identity he so desperately longs for, Temple pretends that he was once a famous gunman. After daily sessions of target practice, he is able to prove his claim with a dazzling display of fancy shooting. His charade works only until a real gunfighter calls his bluff and he must acknowledge the truth. The film attributes Temple's identity crisis in large part to the fact that individual dignity has become dependent on conformity with society's misconceived ideals of human value and success. Temple cannot attain a sense of worth so long as his neighbors consider him nothing more than the humble proprietor of the general store.

The title figure of *Johnny Concho*, played by producer-star Frank Sinatra, compensates for his inferiority complex and cowardice by playing the role of an obnoxious big shot, with his brother close by to shoot anyone who may object. The people tolerate Concho's abusiveness not only because they fear his brother, but more importantly because they depend upon the brother to keep other gunfighters from tearing up the town. The citizens in effect exploit the Concho brothers to maintain the law and order, which they lack the courage and initiative to enforce. When a gunfighter kills Johnny Concho's brother, the townspeople unleash their scorn on Johnny, since there is no longer any reason to have him around. The cowardly Johnny flees; but later, after a preacher helps him straighten out his psyche, he returns to face the gunfighter who killed his brother. In the process, both Johnny and the community learn to face problems honestly rather than create façades that compound rather than eliminate shortcomings. Like *The Fastest Gun Alive, Johnny Concho* ends happily but with a disturbing suggestion that society denies dignity and success to an individual except on terms that discourage honesty to oneself and hence aggravates identity problems.

Westerns, like contemporary social criticism, often associated role-playing and lack of integrity with the desire to get ahead socially, as well as to get along comfortably. The ambitious are characterized by phoniness in their quest for status and power. The social-climbing protagonist of *These Thousand Hills* (1959) is faulted for his affected elitism and snobbish avoidance of former friends rather than for calculated ruthlessness.

The women in some Westerns were also inclined to deny their good instincts and to put on airs for the sake of higher standing. Randolph Scott's girl in *Man in the Saddle* (1952) leaves him to marry a cattle baron only to discover that the adornments of high society cannot replace the genuine affection she had felt for an honest cowboy. In *The Tall Men* (1955), Jane Russell resists the honestly passionate beckonings of Clark Gable, because he wants her to share with him a simple ranch life in contrast with the dazzling future offered her by an ambitious scoundrel (Robert Ryan). Carroll Baker threatens to leave fiancé Gregory Peck in *The Big Country* (1958) because he will not act the role expected of a cattle baron's son-in-law. Peck's role in this film resembles his portrayal of *The Man in the Gray Flannel Suit* (1956), in which he resists his wife's badgering to become a member of the corporate elite.

The uncluttered, straightforward behavior of badmen in several late fifties Westerns made them more attractive characters than many of the good guys at this time. Like the mercenary hero (*Man with the Gun, Warlock*), these badmen feel no compulsion to reform as did the alienated individual of the earlier Westerns. Their threat to society as bandits or killers is never ignored or approved, but it does connote an enviable detachment from the mediocrity of society.

The intended stature of the villain is often clear from the casting of star players. Thus, Audie Murphy as a menacing hired killer in *No Name on the Bullet* (1959) becomes a cynical observer of the hypocrisies and false respectability of those whom he threatens. He finds considerable amusement in taunting certain townspeople whose guilt about previous wrongdoing produces panic when they think Murphy has been contracted to kill them. His presence triggers desperate responses that take the form of a drunken challenge or ugly mob violence. And, in *The Ride Back* (1957), Anthony Quinn plays an outlaw whose life of free love and reckless violence proves to have been more personally fulfilling than that of his captor, a lawman who is tormented by anxieties over having been a perpetual failure.

The film *3:10 to Yuma* (1957) provides a particularly rich

*3:10 to Yuma* (Columbia, 1957). A carefree outlaw held captive by a beleaguered citizen.

contrast between the lifestyle and values of an outlaw and those of a beleaguered but honest citizen. Dan Evans (Van Heflin), a hard-working small rancher who is barely able to support his wife and two boys during a severe drought, is the only man in the community with sufficient backbone and civic responsibility to guard a dangerous outlaw until the train for Yuma prison arrives at the nearest railhead. The captive outlaw, Ben Wade (Glenn Ford), is an amiable scoundrel who is free of any connubial or communal ties and enjoys the lucrative rewards of his trade; but he is a man who will kill with little hesitation to save himself or his gang. In this film, director Delmer Daves interestingly juxtaposes Evans's dispirited family life and strained relations with his wife with a brief but deeply felt romantic interval between Wade and a barroom waitress. With Evans's respectable life there is hardship and marital friction, whereas with Wade's outlawry there is money, freedom, and romance.

As captor and outlaw await the train with the outlaw's gang just around the corner, Ben Wade taunts Dan Evans about the foolishness of risking one's life for a society that will not lift a finger to help, when he could just as well save himself and take part of the holdup money to provide the kind of life his wife deserves. Evans, with obvious strain, withstands the temptations out of a vague sense that man has to do what he has to do. During the climactic confrontation with the gang at the train station, Wade helps Evans to board the train, because he realizes that Evans could justifiably have killed him on several occasions, and he thus feels he must even the score. Since Ben Wade has become such an attractive character, it seems right for the film to suggest that he will escape Yuma prison as he has done in the past. The film ends happily for Evans as well, as he is reconciled with his wife and saved from the drought by a rainstorm. But the earlier scenes of Evans's distress, together with the film's unusually favorable depiction of an unredeemed outlaw, leave the viewer ambivalent as to the relative worth of the socially respectable versus lawless life.

Perhaps no single phenomenon signaling disenchantment with mass society received as much attention in the fifties as did juvenile delinquency. After the Depression, poverty and physical environment were still factors in explaining the waywardness of youth in large urban slums; but it became increasingly evident in the fifties that delinquency was also a middle-class problem. In the words of one commentator, "juvenile delinquency is already creeping from the wrong side of the tracks to the right side."[10] It was common to blame delinquency on nuclear terror, as well as on permissiveness and discord within the family. In 1957 Benjamin Spock felt obliged to revise the 1945 edition of his *Common Sense Book of Baby and Child Care* to place greater emphasis on parental discipline, recognizing obvious failings within the family to properly guide and control children.[11]

Films throughout the fifties similarly interpret delinquency as indicative of middle-class failings and, especially, of family instability. The major youth characters of *Rebel without a Cause* (1955), played by James Dean, Natalie Wood, and Sal Mineo, reflect confusion of values, lack of parental character and guidance, and broken homes in America's middle-class society. The rebellion was not so much against traditional values as against parents' failure to adhere to and pass on those values so their children could properly mature into responsible citizens.

Many postwar Westerns involved the problems of broken families and disturbed youth in troubled, violent times. *Duel in the Sun* (1946), *The Sea of Grass* (1947), *Along the Great Divide* (1951), *Vengeance Valley* (1951), *The Broken Lance* (1954), *The Man from Laramie* (1955), *Gunman's Walk* (1958), *From Hell to Texas* (1958), and *Last Train from Gun Hill* (1959) all are major Westerns in which overbearing fathers and/or motherless families spawn wild or unprincipled offspring who inevitably run afoul of the law. The bad son usually inherits the old man's bullish aggressiveness and scorn for legal authority without the countervailing influence of a virtuous mother or the father's own mature sense of fairness and restraint.[12] Whether

10 Benjamin Fine, *1,000,000 Delinquents* (Cleveland: World Publishing, 1955), p. 27. Selection included in Joseph Satin, ed., *The 1950s: America's Placid Decade* (Boston: Houghton Mifflin, 1960), p. 153.

11 Benjamin Spock, *The Common Sense Book of Baby and Child Care* (New York: Duell, Sloan and Pearce, 1957), p. 2.

12 Only in *Vengeance Valley* (1951) is the rotten son's father a gentle man; here the son's delinquency was due to the lack of a mother and the father's inability to devote enough time to raising him.

the father has spoiled his son or been too rigid with him is less important than are the erroneous or contradictory values reflected in the son's misconduct.

In the few cases where a widowed man rears his youngster successfully, it is assumed that the task is a formidable one. In *The Lone Hand* (1953), the hero wants to marry a pretty neighbor, as much for his young son's benefit as for love. A successful television series, *The Rifleman,* focused on the difficulties, however happily resolved each week, of a widowed father (Chuck Conners) raising his son. These Westerns reaffirm, along with multiple editions of Dr. Spock's manuals, the importance of a healthy nuclear family structure in uncomfortable times. Without love and guidance within a family, young men are susceptible to fall into delinquent or criminal behavior.[13]

Nicholas Ray, who directed two important films on contemporary juvenile delinquency (*Knock on Any Door* [1949], *Rebel without a Cause* [1955]), also dramatized the juvenile problem within the western genre. In *Run for Cover* (1955), Ray cast John Derek (the juvenile delinquent of *Knock on Any Door*) as Davy Bishop, who turns delinquent rather than accept parental care from a reformed gunfighter (James Cagney). The gunfighter-turned-sheriff tries to teach Davy responsibility by making him a deputy; but Davy's rebellious yearning for fast money, together with an inferiority complex over his crippled leg, makes robbing banks a more attractive prospect than the enforcement of law and order. While Davy is clearly to blame for refusing the wisdom and love of his benefactor, his behavior has been conditioned by years of societal neglect. As a ward of the community, Davy had wasted away in the thankless, unpromising job of cowpunching. His desire for greener grass, while dangerously conceived in terms of gunfighting or banditry, is somewhat understandable, given the fruitless nature of his employment.

[13] Westerns that suggest the dangers or actuality of a young man going bad without parents include: *Branded* (1951); *Ambush at Tomahawk Gap* (1953); *The Silver Whip* (1953); *Man without a Star* (1955); *The Rawhide Years* (1956); *Ride a Crooked Trail* (1958); *Saddle the Wind* (1958). The young man usually has some good qualities which, with the help of parents, might have put him on the right path. *Good Day for a Hanging* (1959) is unique in that its delinquent youth is actually a bad person who has manipulated the sympathy of gullible citizens.

He might have made it as a deputy sheriff had he not been crippled by a gun-happy posse of local citizens who mistook him for a train robber. Although Davy eventually exhibits murderous tendencies, director Ray nevertheless suggests that deficiencies in the adult world partially explain, if not excuse, his misconduct.

Run for Cover is less explicit in its indictment of middle-class elders than was Ray's Rebel without a Cause (released the same year) or his The True Story of Jesse James (1957). The latter film was based on Nunnally Johnson's screenplay for Jesse James (1939), which was released by the same studio, Twentieth Century Fox. Screenwriter Walter Neuman and director Nicholas Ray altered the story to make it relevant to the fifties.

With Robert Wagner as Jesse James and Jeffrey Hunter as his brother Frank, director Ray highlighted the theme of juvenile disaffection with the older generation in troubled times. When Jesse voices his discontent and his girlfriend tells him that he is thinking like a child, he replies that he does not like the way grownups think. His search for love, peace, and security is frustrated by a society that is divided by postwar animosities and preoccupied with material gain. When he is shot during the Civil War while surrendering under a flag of truce, an act suggesting adult treachery, a neighbor refuses to aid him for fear of being labeled a Confederate sympathizer and losing everything he has worked for. This same neighbor later refuses to give his daughter's hand in marriage to Jesse until he proves that he can provide for her. Money is more important to the nagging adult than is love. After Jesse begins his career as a robber, he collects his girl and disdainfully hands her father a bag of loot in exchange.

Youth again upstages adult when Jesse assumes the identity of a prospering businessman and takes his bride househunting: when an eager landlord tries to rent them a place, Jesse mockingly tells him that a nude painting on the wall offends their sensibilities. The man is overjoyed at the prospect of having such "genteel" folk move in, because "It'll raise property values." Nicholas Ray had directed a similar scene in Rebel without a Cause, where James Dean and Natalie Wood fantasize being a high-brow, married couple who are house shopping, with Sal Mineo parodying the solicitous landlord.

Despite his scorn for the adult world, Jesse James holds to its basic values. Defiance of legal authority brings only temporary gratification and soon becomes self-destructive and futile. He finally tells his wife that after one more job he will retire, invest in a good business, and raise a family. As with Ray's *Rebel without a Cause,* the alienated youth rebels not against middle-class values but against the failure of adults to live honestly by those values.

Aside from its stress on juvenile rebelliousness, *The True Story of Jesse James* also differed from its 1939 predecessor in relating Jesse's lawlessness to bitterness and recriminations that divided communities during and after the Civil War. *Jesse James* (1939) had explained outlawry as a reaction against greedy capitalists (represented by the railroad) who exploited poor folk after the Civil War, in much the same way as the heartless bankers portrayed by Steinbeck had displaced poor farmers during the Depression. It was commonplace during the fifties to blame juvenile delinquency upon the Cold War and a general atmosphere of domestic and international violence. While Americans fought in Korea, Senator McCarthy and the government were breeding fear and distrust over the alleged dangers of subversion. John Cogley wrote in *Commonweal* (1955) that juvenile delinquents, with their casual indulgence in rape, murder, and sadism, were products of an age that treasured violence and rewarded brutality: "We cannot have wars and injustice and hope thereby to gain the fruits of peace and justice."[14]

The relationship between delinquency and a violent society is also central to Arthur Penn's *The Left-Handed Gun* (1958), a highly stylized version of the Billy the Kid legend based on a play by Gore Vidal. Paul Newman as Billy is a brooding, inarticulate lad whose boyish charm and spontaneous foolery can erupt into uncontrollable violence. Director Penn described his Billy in an interview as infantile and "almost psychopathic" in coping with everyday injustices.[15] Billy's obsession with avenging his employer's slaying in turn unleashes the underlying brutality

14 Satin, ed., *The 1950s,* p. 15.
15 Eric Sherman and Martin Rubin, *The Director's Event: Interviews with Five American Film-Makers* (New York: Signet Books, 1969), p. 122.

*Jesse James* (Twentieth Century Fox, 1939). The James brothers as Depression-era farm boys.

*The True Story of Jesse James* (Twentieth Century Fox, 1957). The James brothers as fifties teenagers.

of supposedly respectable citizens. When he shoots the crooked lawmen who murdered his employer, the townspeople attack, burn, and ransack the house of a rancher who has befriended him. Their act of vengeance appears even more vicious and senseless than Billy's individual killings. Later, as Billy awaits execution in jail, people gather from miles around for the thrill of watching him hang. A little girl is later seen giggling at the corpse of a deputy Billy has slain while escaping. When lawman Pat Garrett finally kills Billy, it is at best a necessary means of restoring the veneer of peace that protects a violent society from itself.

Still another troubled-youth variation of the Billy the Kid legend is *One Eyed Jacks* (1961). Marlon Brando stars as the brooding, sensitive Rio, a more stable and sane character than Paul Newman's Billy the Kid. Rio plots to ruin a sheriff, Dad Longworth (Karl Malden), who as a partner in crime had betrayed him to the Mexican authorities. The outlaw's integrity contrasts with the lawman-citizen's treachery and deceit. Their respective social positions are the reverse side of their true characters, each, therefore, being a "one eyed jack."

The film's story and characterizations pose the familiar conflict of rebellious, romantic youth versus the hypocritical, two-faced elder. Although *One Eyed Jacks* ends with Rio's having a change of heart regarding his intent to kill Dad Longworth, there is no indication that Rio has the desire or will to become a responsible citizen. He will evidently care for the sheriff's daughter, who bears his child; but his final ride into the sunset suggests a continuance of romantic individualism divorced from any formal association with the existing social order.

Not all adolescent characters in Westerns after World War II are troubled or rebellious. Nor was Philip French entirely correct when he wrote that "the Western assumes . . . young people have a lot to learn from their elders and very little to teach them."[16] Certainly, in many Westerns a young man lacked the maturity to handle a gun (*Run for Cover* [1955], *Man without a Star* [1955], *Gunman's Walk* [1958], among others) or

[16] French, *Westerns,* p. 69.

naïvely condemned his father as a killer when in reality he had had a reason to kill (*River of No Return* [1954], *Gun Glory* [1957], *The Lonely Man* [1957]). But in other Westerns, such as *Red River* (1948), *Three Young Texans* (1954), *Track of the Cat* (1954), *The Broken Lance* (1954), *The Burning Hills* (1956), *Backlash* (1956), *The Halliday Brand* (1957), and *Flaming Star* (1960), a representative of the younger generation acted more commendably than did much of the adult world. *Red River, The Halliday Brand,* and *Track of the Cat* pit good offspring against wrongheaded parent or guardian; whereas *The Broken Lance, The Burning Hills,* and *Flaming Star* target corruption and other social weaknesses outside the family. Rather than being rebellious delinquents, the young heroes of these films function in a responsible manner—according to the traditional western motif—to correct evils perpetrated by their elders.

*The Broken Lance* stands out among these and most other Westerns of the fifties in the nature of its social criticism. Young Joe Devereaux (Robert Wagner), the devoted son of cattle baron Matt Devereaux (Spencer Tracy), matures to adulthood at a time when the new urban social order is gradually displacing an open frontier dominated by strong individualists like his father. Joe exhibits his father's warmth and individualism but without the brutish stubbornness that has come to him with advancing age. As Matt wages a losing battle to prevent a mining company from polluting his water resources, the tragic implications of advancing civilization become clear. The eventual demise of Matt Devereaux and, by implication, of an entire frontier era spells the triumph of unscrupulous economic and political interests, with all the hypocrisy, opportunism, and racism that characterizes the modern urban society. It is this society that Joe is left to cope with as he rides off with his bride to start a new life.

*The Broken Lance* set an early precedent for the sixties Westerns of Sam Peckinpah and other filmmakers, who are credited with revising the western myth in accordance with contemporary political and social disenchantment. Peckinpah would juxtapose both young (*Pat Garrett and Billy the Kid*) and old (*The Wild Bunch*) frontier individualists in a losing fight against the urban-corporate establishment. If his heroes were more disreputable

*The Broken Lance* (Twentieth Century Fox, 1954). A confrontation with the racism and duplicity of society.

or alienated than were the Devereauxs, they share a common distaste for modern civilization.

Westerns of the 1960s would offer less a new picture of society than one that would accentuate the societal viciousness and banality depicted in the fifties Westerns and would glorify less ambiguously the hero's violence and alienation. This in turn renders questionable the tendency of many historians to interpret the disenchantment of the sixties as a sudden departure from what they presume to be a decade of public apathy and contentment. The social criticism in Westerns of the fifties suggests that, even though Americans at that time were less inclined to riot or protest, they were nonetheless aware of, and disturbed by, the shortcomings of their society.

CHAPTER SEVEN

AGAINST THE ESTABLISHMENT

N OTING BOTH THE RECENT DE-
cline of movie and television Westerns and the scholarly skepticism of Frederick Jackson Turner's assumptions concerning the
frontier's inspirational quality, John Higham wrote in the late
sixties, "It is necessary to ask if today's Americans are losing
Turner's underlying faith in the relevance of the pioneer heritage."[1] Pauline Kael in 1974 concluded that the Hollywood Western had disappeared in favor of two-fisted reactionaries like
Buford Pusser and Dirty Harry battling modern crime and corruption: "A few more Westerns may still straggle in, but the
Western is dead."[2]

Although Westerns had declined in number since their zenith
of popularity during the 1950s, until recently they were one of
the few genres to survive as the motion picture industry muddled
through its most precarious financial era. In his study of Hollywood films during the sixties, John Baxter argued that the industry relied on the wide audience appeal of "Westerns, gangster
dramas, [and] wise-cracking comedies."[3] Baxter's paperback publication even sported a cover photo of John Wayne spanking
Maureen O'Hara in the western comedy *McLintock,* highlighting the importance of Westerns during the sixties.

More significant than the quantitative trend in Westerns have
been the thematic alterations that have taken place since the

[1] John Higham, *Writing American History* (Bloomington: Indiana University Press, 1970), p. 127.
[2] *The New Yorker,* 25 February 1974, p. 100.
[3] John Baxter, *Hollywood in the Sixties* (New York: A. S. Barnes, 1972),
p. 10.

fifties in accordance with the changing intellectual and political climate. The polarization of politics, reflected in the presidential candidacies of Barry Goldwater and George Wallace from the right and George McGovern from the left, was accompanied by a similar dichotomy between the obviously conservative Westerns of John Wayne and the liberal-left criticisms of such directors as Arthur Penn and Robert Altman. Whatever the perspective, most Westerns shared a profound disenchantment with the institutions and mainstream values of American society, comparable to the eroding faith in the liberal center as reflected in prominent intellectual and political positions. Frontier individualism, whether threatened or reactionary, assumed added importance given the dubious merits and prospects of the larger society.

Several major Westerns boasting the traditional notion of a progressive, frontier America where strong individuals fought for the good democratic society made a strong showing during the Kennedy years of the "new frontier." As if to rekindle the pride in America's frontier heritage that had begun to wane in movies since World War II, MGM filled the nation's Cinerama screens with the most lavish Western spectacle to date, *How the West Was Won* (1962). Veteran screenwriter James Webb wrote the script, while the equally seasoned Henry Hathaway, George Marshall, and John Ford directed segments of this epic chronicle of heroic pioneers conquering the wilderness to build a new nation. The film's tremendous success at the box office suggests that there remained an audience for the traditional optimistic vision of the frontier epoch, although Hollywood chose not to follow this motif in the subsequent years when widespread turmoil and dissension overshadowed whatever unanimity and hopefulness had been established during the Kennedy years.

With *The Alamo* (1960), *North to Alaska* (1960), and *The Comancheros* (1961), John Wayne began the decade with his inimitable brand of tough frontier wisdom. As director and star of his own Batjak Company's *The Alamo,* Wayne paid tribute to the brave Texans who died for freedom against Mexican despotism. Unlike so many Westerns of the fifties and sixties, there is no suggestion of anxiety-ridden individuals or of a weak, complacent, corrupt society. In *The Alamo* people lived the good, wholesome life and were strong enough to preserve that life against tyranny.

As an enterprising prospector in *North to Alaska* and a duty-conscious Texas ranger in *The Comancheros,* under the direction of Hollywood veterans Henry Hathaway and Michael Curtiz respectively, Wayne's inevitable triumph over villainous obstructions to justice and progress accompanied a robust, good-natured comic style, which most critics belatedly noted in *True Grit* (1969). A dash of comic self-parody softened the more abrasive features of his ruggedly domineering image. Another character would often upbraid Wayne to counter his accentuated stubbornness or righteousness. Thus, Stuart Whitman as a prisoner in *The Comancheros* (1961), after being unduly humiliated by the over-confident Wayne, clobbers him with a shovel. Heroines, like Angie Dickinson in *Rio Bravo* (1959), Capucine in *North to Alaska,* and Maureen O'Hara in *McLintock* (1963) commonly protested or corrected Wayne's occasional bullheadedness. Yet these character traits remained minor and even endearing flaws in contrast with the violent dementedness of Wayne's character in *Red River* (1948) and *The Searchers* (1956). Throughout the sixties, Wayne conspicuously avoided playing the seriously alienated loner whose psychological and social adjustment was necessary to reconcile individualism with the greater good. Whatever divided Wayne from society in his sixties Westerns implied not his but society's maladjustment.

With the possible exception of *The Sons of Katie Elder* (1965), in which he makes amends for his irresponsible gun-slinging days and rejoins society, Wayne's films of the sixties (after 1961) counterposed his rugged individualism with a bland or sometimes corrupt social order. Particularly when directed by Andrew McLaglen, Wayne's screen personality became closely aligned with his well-publicized conservative politics. In McLaglen's *McLintock* (1963) and *Chisum* (1970), Wayne played the self-made, successful cattleman and respected patriarch of the community. Unlike Westerns of the late forties and early fifties (*Duel in the Sun* [1946], *Sea of Grass* [1947], *Red River* [1948], and

*The Furies* [1950]), *McLintock* and *Chisum* posed no conflict between the frontier aristocrat and the public welfare but assumed that the good society is really a product of the efforts of the untrammeled great man. The cattleman fought hard for his domain and in the process brought civilization to the West. No apology was needed to justify his deserved position of leadership and material status. Only *The Broken Lance* (1954) and *Ten Wanted Men* (1955) had approached this position during the fifties, whereas most Westerns (*Tribute to a Bad Man* [1956], *The Halliday Brand* [1957], *The Man from Laramie* [1955]) continued to emphasize the abuse of power by the big rancher.

A favorite theme in Westerns had been the conflict between ranchers and homesteaders, where justice demanded that the powerful ranch baron abandon his arbitrariness in favor of the new democratic order of common settlers. *McLintock,* on the other hand, showed the homesteaders being misled by a conniving land agent into believing they had a legal right to some of the land claimed by cattle baron Wayne. In essence the land agent is the liberal bureaucrat who pursues his own selfish interests by giving the people empty promises of something for nothing by taking from the successful rich. McLintock (Wayne) justifies his ownership by right of conquest and argues that nobody ever gave anyone anything; the homesteaders are mistaken if they think they can easily establish homes and survive the hazards of the open range. What has been properly earned cannot be usurped by grasping bureaucrats and an undeserving populace.

Wayne again defends private enterprise against bureaucratic intrusion in Andrew McLaglen's *The Undefeated* (1969). As a veteran of the Civil War, Wayne declines to reenlist and explains to the Union commander that he and his men deserve to make an honest dollar after fighting for their country. Moreover, the country will benefit from his private venture, which involves selling horses to the Army. But later, when the government insists on buying the horses at an unfairly low price, Wayne has no qualms about selling them instead to Maximilian's forces in Mexico, who have made a reasonably competitive offer. The two shifty-eyed U.S. buyers question Wayne's patriotism for not put-

*The Undefeated* (Twentieth Century Fox, 1969). A defender of private enterprise.

ting his country above profit. Angered, Wayne replies with a stiff punch. Just economic reward for the entrepreneur is presumably the greatest of self-evident truths.

While McLaglen's Westerns centered on Wayne as the respected laissez-faire advocate. Henry Hathaway's adaptation of Charles Porter's best-selling *True Grit* (1969) supported Wayne's tough-mindedness about law and order. Wayne's broadly comical exaggerations of Marshal Rooster Cogburn's surly character did not negate the sincerity of the contrast between this honorable, rugged individual and an unappreciative, settled society. Instead of thanking Cogburn for capturing notorious outlaws, the town court righteously questions his being too quick to kill his quarry rather than bringing them to trial. The same society that condemns Cogburn's violent ways is seen early in the film turning a public hanging into a festive celebration. Cogburn and his spunky employer, Matty Ross (Kim Darby), discover in each other that rare quality of "true grit" apparently lacking in most people.[4]

*The War Wagon* (1967), *Big Jake* (1972), and *The Train Robbers* (1973) also found Wayne purposely aloof from a society with which he held little in common. *The Train Robbers* even concluded with Wayne riding off to rob a train after a Wells Fargo agent had allowed him to be swindled. Howard Hawks starred Wayne in *El Dorado* (1967) and *Rio Lobo* (1971), both virtual remakes of *Rio Bravo* (1959), where law and order depends upon professionalism in wielding a gun. The hero of Hawks's films stands with his professional colleagues between order and chaos, with little direct reliance upon the larger society.

If Wayne did not succumb to the cynicism and despair of the late-sixties Westerns that attacked a violent and corrupt frontier society, it is nonetheless significant that his character stood apart from that society and protected it less for its worth or potential than for his own personal code of honor. The individual-societal harmony idealized in such films as *Red River, Hondo,* and *The Searchers,* where Wayne ultimately submitted to the societal

---

[4] Wayne repeated his tough-lawman role in *Rooster Cogburn* (1975), with Katharine Hepburn playing an older version of Matty Ross. Rooster (Wayne) nearly loses his badge for defying judicial restraints against killing outlaws but proves indispensable in preserving law and order.

march of progress, was no longer a major theme in many of his sixties and seventies Westerns. Even the focus of his law-and-order themes (*True Grit, El Dorado*) was on the importance of mutual respect between Wayne and friend(s) or Wayne and enemies as opposed to the issue of societal progress or failure.

Andrew McLaglen, who filmed some of Wayne's more conservative Westerns, remained conspicuously traditional and optimistic in his other Westerns.[5] *The Way West* (1967) involves personally flawed but hardy pioneers who are led by a neurotic but enlightened Kirk Douglas in blazing a new trail to Oregon. The way is plagued more by interpersonal conflicts in the psychosexual manner of *Peyton Place* than by external dangers, but Bronislau Kaper's title song and score continually remind the audience of the grand, heroic achievement that is taking place. *The Ballad of Josie* (1968) is a family comedy with Doris Day fighting a greedy landowner for her ranch and leading the local women's suffrage movement. Doris wins both battles, but concludes that it is best not to carry women's rights too far and risk losing a good man along with the joys of home and family. McLaglen's humor is earthier but no less innocuous in *Something Big* (1971), in which an amiable outlaw (Dean Martin) is reformed by a pretty Scottish lassie.

The upbeat tone of Wayne's triumphant individualism and McLaglen's view of the West, like the march-of-progress theme in *How the West Was Won,* ran counter to most other Westerns of the sixties and seventies. John Higham speculated that the concluding scenes of *How the West Was Won* reflected an "incapacity on the part of the producers to believe in what they were saying." A panorama of modern freeways hardly seemed an apt symbol for the wonderful civilization that had been carved from primitive wilderness, especially following nearly three hours of magnificent scenery and monumental feats of valor.[6] Yet Higham's observation tells more about the intellectual's alarm at America's urban chaos than it does about the film itself. There is

---

[5] *Bandolero* (1968) is McLaglen's only Western to end tragically for the heroes. But even here the heroes are good badmen in the style of classic Westerns. The early scenes show the seamier side of a frontier town, but the final villainy comes in the form of Mexican bandits rather than a corrupt society.

[6] Higham, *Writing American History,* p. 127.

little in *How the West Was Won* to dispute the sincerity of its vision of modern progress, however incongruous with liberal thinking.

The choice of symbols nevertheless seems curious, if only because Westerns themselves by 1963 had begun to depict the modern urban civilization as empty and dehumanizing in contrast with the dying frontier world of the freedom-loving individualist. Cowboys, adventurers, and lawmen who had once found fulfillment as self-sufficient individuals became forgotten anachronisms, as an institutionalized, confining urban order replaced the open frontier.

James Fenimore Cooper had used a similar format in dramatizing Natty Bumpo's retreat before the modern order he had helped to forge; and William S. Hart, in *Tumbleweeds* (1926), sentimentalized the fate of the cowboy as settlers moved in to occupy the open cattle ranges. In these cases, however, convictions about the inevitability and desirability of progress countered sadness over the disappearance of old ways and values. Hart senses the loss of the cowboy epoch but accepts and presumably adapts to the new order.

During the 1960s the theme of a declining frontier individualism involved a more disparaging outlook toward modern times. The frontier environment of individual freedom and spontaneity becomes less a precedent for a necessarily more structured, progressive civilization than a happier alternative to the confining, depersonalizing social order of today.

*The Misfits* (1961), *Lonely Are the Brave* (1962), *The Man Who Shot Liberty Valence* (1962), *Ride the High Country* (1962), and *Hud* (1963) examine the confrontation between Western individualists and the forces of modernization. The cowboy heroes of *The Misfits* and *Lonely Are the Brave* are proud men who desperately cling to fading remnants of the great outdoors and a way of life free of the intrusions of an increasingly urban, mechanized society.

Gay Langland (Clark Gable) in *The Misfits* prefers wrangling wild horses in the wide-open spaces to working for wages amid the vulgarity of Reno, Nevada. Yet changing times have transformed this once wholesome endeavor into one of senseless cruelty. The formerly prolific herds of wild horses have dwindled so that wrangling now connotes mere destructiveness. Where there had once been a market for riding horses, Gay must now sell his captive horses to dog food canneries. The individual dignity of the hard-working man on horseback has given way to the mechanized nastiness of small planes swooping down on frightened animals.

*Lonely Are the Brave* opens with a lone cowboy, Jack Burns (Kirk Douglas), reclining under the clear sky over a vast desert, obviously at peace with himself and his faithful horse. A jet suddenly streaks overhead, the first of many images symbolizing the intrusion of modern times on the serenity of Burns's lifestyle. The scene is a twentieth-century version of the blast of the train whistle interrupting Nathaniel Hawthorne's pastoral idyll at Sleepy Hollow. Burns, unable to compromise his need for freedom even for the woman he loves, remains a tragic victim of an encroaching social order from which death is the only escape.

Unlike his friend Paul, who prefers to sit out an unjust prison sentence for the sake of a safe and respectable future for himself and his family, Burns heroically battles his legal pursuers and all their technological resources. The sheriff (Walter Matthau) can only admire Burns's bravado and secretly hope that he will make it safely to Mexico. Burns and his life are, after all, the antithesis of the sheriff and his tedious, regulated life as a colorless civil servant. At the end of the film, the sheriff beholds sadly the dying Burns, whose escape on horseback has been terminated by a truck skidding on a rain-splattered highway.

The title character of *Hud* (Paul Newman) is also a restless, straightforward, and individualistic cowboy who is confronted with the shoddiness that is the modern West. But his aversion to the drab, empty environment has caused Hud, unlike Gay Langland or Jack Burns, to become morally corrupt. While his father doggedly maintains a sense of dignity and honor from the old days, Hud is a man without scruples, a bitterly cynical and selfish lout. Yet, as his nephew reminds his grandfather, "Why pick on Hud, Grandpa? Nearly everybody around town is like him."[7]

[7] Pauline Kael, *I Lost It at the Movies* (New York: Bantam Books, 1966), p. 83.

*Lonely Are the Brave* (Universal, 1962). Flight from entrapment by modern society.

John Ford, who in *Sergeant Rutledge* (1960) and *Two Rode Together* (1961) exhibited a more critical view of America's pioneer society than in his earlier Westerns, in *The Man Who Shot Liberty Valence* (1962) offered a melancholy and troubling statement regarding the civilization of the West. Ford seemed more concerned with what had been lost than with what had been won as a wild western town entered the modern era. He acknowledged the bravery, idealism, and accomplishments of a young lawyer, Ransom Stoddard (James Stewart), who arouses civic responsibility against lawlessness in the town and who as a politician brings this final remnant of the Wild West into the modern age. However, Ford clearly mourns the decline of the archetypal frontier individualist.

The antithesis of Stoddard is Tom Doniphon (John Wayne), a violent hero of the plains whose status of respect and honor in the community is being undermined by the modern order. Doniphon recognizes the inevitability of change, however, and supports it. He appears to have accepted stoically his own fadeout into anonymity, as he withholds from the town the fact that it was he and not Stoddard who actually shot Liberty Valance. To have done otherwise would have ruined Stoddard's campaign image and would have endangered what little good accompanied the inevitable progress of America. Stoddard himself knows who actually shot the gunman and thus can never be entirely at ease with being credited in his political career as the man who brought civilization to the West. In the final scene, Stoddard and his wife (Vera Miles) ponder this unsettling truth as their train crosses the grassy plains, and the film ends on a note of sadness and loss.

If *The Man Who Shot Liberty Valence* was not as explicitly critical of contemporary culture as were *The Misfits* and *Lonely Are the Brave,* it nevertheless shared with those films a sentimental attachment to individualism and a regret over the loss of and disregard for individualism in a changing America. Sam Peckinpah achieved his first critical recognition with a similar theme in *Ride the High Country* (1962), released within a month of *Lonely Are the Brave* and *The Man Who Shot Liberty Valence.*

Randolph Scott and Joel McCrea made their final notable

film appearance in *Ride the High Country* as former lawmen who are reunited to guard a mine payroll. Both were once admired and respected for their heroic town taming and now suffer the humiliations of anonymity and menial jobs. When Steve Judd (Joel McCrea) expresses disappointment at the smallness of the payroll he is to guard, his employer disinterestedly explains that the days of the forty-niners have given way to the day of the steady businessman.

The movie's theme is set when old Judd wanders into town and thinks the crowds that line the street are there to pay homage to his services in taming the West. But he is hustled off the street first by a motorcar and then by a pompously uniformed policeman. The town has gathered not to honor its heroes but to enjoy a tawdry camel race and carnival. Despite the feelings of his partner Gil Westrum (Randolph Scott) that they should steal the payroll and enjoy some reward for their years of self-sacrifice, Judd stays true to his code of honor. Now in his late years, he can feel prepared to "enter my house justified." When challenged to a final shootout to protect a young girl—the only aspect of civilization worth saving—both men unite in a final blaze of glory and at last transcend their insignificance in the changing frontier.

This sympathetic portrait of aging individuals threatened by the encroachment of a new social order is reiterated in such later Peckinpah films as *The Wild Bunch* (1969) and *The Ballad of Cable Hogue* (1970), but with variations that correspond with the more disparaging intellectual and political criticism of the late sixties. The aging, underemployed heroes of *Ride the High Country,* like Gay Langland (*The Misfits*), Jack Burns (*Lonely Are the Brave*), Hud's grandfather (*Hud*), and Tom Doniphon (*The Man Who Shot Liberty Valence*) are the discards of modern societal progress upon whom the Kennedy-Johnson administrations would shower unemployment benefits and medicare. Their plight is, in part, economic but, even more, emotional and spiritual; it derives more from a sense of lost dignity, respect, and honor than from material deprivation.

Certainly the most heralded and influential exposé of how modern progress had eluded many Americans, Michael Harrington's *The Other America* was published in 1962, the same year in which *Lonely Are the Brave, Ride the High Country,* and *The Man Who Shot Liberty Valence* were released. While the films lack Harrington's blatantly reformist posture, they reflect the same concern for the humiliation and degradation of those deprived of a meaningful job and social position by virtue of obsolete skills and/or age. Gil Restrum, in his proud resentment at having nothing to show for his years as a lawman, suffers what Harrington calls the "special degradation" of those deprived of dignified work or social respect because "they had passed the line of human obsolescence in this industrial society."[8]

The Kennedy-Johnson response to the kinds of problems outlined by Harrington was overshadowed by the war in Vietnam and the outbreak of urban racial disturbances. Campus protestors, New Left intellectuals, and other critics of American society not only decried the inequalities and dehumanization of postwar urban industrial development, but increasingly attributed the nation's ills to the "establishment"—a government-corporate complex of political and business elites who dominated national affairs. Herbert Marcuse and Theodore Roszak among other intellectuals speculated about the failures of the technocratic society and the need for an alternative social structure and vision; the liberal-capitalist tradition had created war and oppression overseas and had repressed freedom and equality at home.[9]

Movies in general and Westerns in particular became more critical in their vision of society, more pessimistic about reform, and more accepting of personal violence as an alternative, rather than a solution, to social vapidity. Westerns of the late sixties and early seventies gave popular expression to growing intellectual and political reservations about corporate domination of American society.

In *The Wild Bunch* (1969), Sam Peckinpah repeated the theme from *Ride the High Country,* of proud individuals over-

[8] Michael Harrington, *The Other America: Poverty in the United States* (Baltimore: Penguin Books, Inc., 1973), p. 27.

[9] Herbert Marcuse, *One-Dimensional Man: Studies in the Ideology of Advanced Industrial Society* (Boston: Beacon Press, 1966). Theodore Roszak, *The Making of a Counter Culture: Reflections on the Technocratic Society and Its Youthful Opposition* (Garden City, N.Y.: Anchor Books, 1969).

come by changing times, but with the added ingredient of a corrupt corporate establishment. Given the late sixties' atmosphere of dissidence and confrontation, Peckinpah appropriately focused on outlaws who are violently at odds with a new social order that eschews personal freedom. His outlaws bear little resemblance to the populist Robin Hoods of late-thirties and early-forties Westerns or to the misunderstood, youthful rebels of the fifties. They are violent men who rob for profit and for the enjoyment of a particular lifestyle within a vacuous and even more violent civilization.

George Roy Hill's *Butch Cassidy and the Sundance Kid,* released the same year as *The Wild Bunch,* similarly depicts outlaws who are trying to preserve a way of life in the early twentieth century against the increasingly effective law enforcement that is generated by the railroad. Director Hill romantically views the defeat of Butch and Sundance by an expanding civilization as a death of frolicsome innocence. Butch Cassidy (Paul Newman) has never killed as an outlaw, and he is repulsed when he must do so in a legal capacity.

By contrast, Peckinpah emphasized man's violent nature, so that the defeat of the Ballard gang suggests the triumph of modern, institutionalized violence over the western brand of individual violence. *The Wild Bunch* contains no romantic interludes of "raindrops falling on my head" to suggest boyish innocence on the part of his badmen, but shows them as hardened, violent men, whose sole virture lies in their sense of personal honor and mutual loyalty. The railroad enforcer, however, is totally without scruples, as he allows the slaughter of innocent citizens in the process of ambushing the Ballard gang and then organizes a posse of bloodthirsty rabble.[10]

The contemporary relevance of Peckinpah's outlaw theme

[10] See ch. 3 for the critical implications of Peckinpah's *The Wild Bunch* (1969) and *Major Dundee* (1965) regarding contemporary antiwar notions. With respect to the nation's domestic turbulence on campuses and city streets during the sixties, films like *The Wild Bunch* and *Butch Cassidy and the Sundance Kid* reflect not so much the value and purpose of protesting national policy as a view that touches upon the underlying disenchantment with established social values and institutions that made a potentially violent confrontation acceptable.

became even more obvious in *Pat Garrett and Billy the Kid* (1973). With Kris Kristofferson as Billy and Bob Dylan as his groupie, the counter-culture overtones of youthful dissident battling an adult establishment are unmistakable. Billy and his hippy-like pals long to be free to do their own thing—such as shooting the heads off roosters and chasing wild turkeys—but are tragically silenced by politically powerful cattle interests. Billy is hounded and killed because his refusal to conform threatens the legal order that protects and enriches the local and state power structure. Pat Garrett has conformed in return for the peace and security that becomes important with age. Yet the price of compromising with the system is nothing less than Garrett's personal honor and self-respect. That in killing Billy for the "law" Garrett has also killed himself is a point driven home when Garrett shoots at his own mirror image after shooting Billy.

As with the protagonists in *The Wild Bunch,* Peckinpah does not cover up or justify the violent inclinations of Billy the Kid. What he does suggest is that the Westerner at least killed in accordance with a code of honor related to personal pride and dignity, whereas the modern legal establishment licensed wholesale killings with hypocritical pieties about social order and progress.

Director Stan Dragoti's *Dirty Little Billy* presents a far less glamorous portrayal of the famous outlaw. In place of the smooth good looks and magnetic charm of Kristofferson's Billy is the sniveling, filthy runt portrayed by Michael J. Pollard. Yet the film suggests that Billy as a young man had little chance in life once his stern stepfather brought the family to a squalid town in the West. After his stepfather's death, Billy's mother immediately takes up residence with the town's leading capitalist promoter, who is filling his own pockets by attracting settlers to this grim locale on the dubious premise that they can here build a new and prosperous life. Early in the film the promoter calls a town meeting and draws cheers with the good news that an epidemic has taken forty or fifty lives in a nearby town and has driven the survivors to this town, thus providing a population sufficient to request a peace officer. Dragoti's alteration of the traditional notion of a progressive American civilization is clear from the film's opening image of a train belching smoke everywhere as it approaches a muddy town.

*Bad Company* (1972) focuses on the tragi-comic experiences of a young draft evader and a band of young dropouts as they rob their way across the empty plains. At one point in the film, the group meets a settler heading his wagon back east after having discovered that the West is not the land of promise. Released the same year, *The Great Northfield Minnesota Raid* retells the saga of the James and Younger boys in contemporary terms of ragged nonconformists who take on the hypocritical establishment. The propensity of Cole Younger (Cliff Robertson) for mystical visions, together with his being a social dropout, strongly suggest the counter-culture alternative to accepted behavioral norms.

Other Westerns, such as *Welcome to Hard Times* (1967), *Firecreek* (1968), and *McCabe and Mrs. Miller* (1971), showed the failure of individual enterprise in grim frontier towns devoid of communal solidarity and tending toward deterioration or corporate tyranny. The heroes of *Welcome to Hard Times* and *Firecreek,* played by Henry Fonda and James Stewart respectively, are admitted failures, having faded into quiet seclusion in isolated, backward settlements. In both films gunmen threaten the townspeople, who lack the courage and determination to defend themselves. Despite a thematic resemblance between these films and *High Noon,* the towns lack the prosperity and promise of Hadleyville, and they have no one of the caliber of Marshal Kane to save them. In *Firecreek,* Stewart eventually works up the courage to combat the villains single-handedly, but otherwise he is painfully aware that he has wasted away as an individual.

There are no grand heroics in *Welcome to Hard Times.* In fact, the film suggests that individual bravado with a gun is ultimately futile and self-destructive. Only a determined effort on the part of the entire community can build up its shabby town and thus assure its survival against crazed gunmen. The film remains ambiguous, however, as to whether this will ever be accomplished. Offsetting the enthusiasm of the film's central character (Henry Fonda) for rebuilding the town of Hard Times is the selfish and defeatist attitude of the other citizens.

In direct contrast with Fonda's communal ideals is the self-interest of McCabe in *McCabe and Mrs. Miller,* a film that details the efforts of an enterprising, nonheroic type to build a house of prostitution into a thriving business. McCabe (Warren Beatty) represents a mock version of the small businessman whose initiative Americans have traditionally considered to be the backbone of the nation's growth and progress. His business does become the basis for a growing community, but director Robert Altman, like Sam Peckinpah and other filmmakers of the time, proceeds to show that the future of America lay not with the individual but with the corrupt and indomitable corporation.

Hirelings of a big mining company eventually kill McCabe, after he refuses to sell a share of his business. Among scenes of the gunbattle between McCabe and his killers, Altman has interspersed scenes of the townspeople, oblivious to McCabe's plight and death, scrambling to put out a fire in the church, which up to that point had had little importance in their lives. The church will remain a part of the town's future but, like everything else, as an adjunct to the ruling corporation. The scene strongly suggests Herbert Marcuse's thesis of the "one-dimensional man," whereby modern society is no longer conscious of distinctions to be made between "immediate" and "real" interest.[11] Equally hopeless is McCabe's decision to fight the company strongarms, given the corporate nature of social progress. Mrs. Miller (Julie Christie), unlike McCabe, knows he cannot buck the company; she retires to an opium den to grasp the mental oblivion the townspeople are gulled into accepting.

The title character of Frank Perry's *Doc* (1971) likewise withdraws to the opium den to seek temporary relief from the agonies of living in a violent, corrupt world. This latest and most despairing version of the Wyatt Earp/Doc Holliday friendship and their battle with the Clantons in Tombstone presents Earp as an opportunist whose respectable family-man image and campaign for law and order disguise personal ambitions for status and power. Holliday is still the tubercular, moody gambler he was in such famous blockbusters as John Ford's *My Darling*

---

[11] Marcuse, *One-Dimensional Man,* pp. xiii–xiv.

*McCabe and Mrs. Miller* (Warner Bros., 1971). Townspeople attend to a burning church instead of the more important danger of corporate domination.

*Clementine* and John Sturges's *Gunfight at the O.K. Corral,* but he is no longer playing second fiddle to Earp's heroic figure. In *Doc,* Holliday's alienation is not a psychological aberration, but a conscious rejection of the violence and corruption that characterize Earp's kind of respectability.

The heroic image of Earp had already been mildly revised by Sturges in *Hour of the Gun* (1967) to suggest a susceptibility to violent behavior, as Earp went gunning for the Clantons in a ruthless, vengeful way that overrode considerations of social justice or even fair play. As the figure of Earp declined from heroism to opportunistic conformity with a corrupt establishment or to episodes of arbitrary violence, Judge Roy Bean, another well-known Westerner, rose from despotic villainy to heroic nonconformism. Whereas in *The Westerner* (1940) Bean (Walter Brennan) had ruthlessly obstructed settlers from civilizing the West, in *The Life and Times of Judge Roy Bean* (1972) he (played by Paul Newman) does battle with the new civilization, which is dominated by greedy oil exploiters.

Disillusionment with a violent and purposeless civilization led the heroes of *The Appaloosa* (1966) and *The Hired Hand* (1971) back to the humble agrarian life they had once rejected. Although the simple pursuits of horse raising and farming are potentially more hopeful than an opium den, they nevertheless represent a rejection of the social mainstream. The quiet yeoman's life, with family and a plot of land, offers the inner tranquility and fulfillment absent in the outside world.

*The Appaloosa* and *The Hired Hand* idealize a kind of domestic commitment missing in most Westerns of the period. But they differ from the classic western lyricism of the great outdoors (e.g., *Shane*) by removing any connotation of a promising civilization. The ideal becomes resignation to familial responsibility and honest toil rather than laying the groundwork for a progressive society.

Films like *Welcome to Hard Times* and *Doc* attacked the idea that the frontier had been the free environment Peckinpah and other filmmakers assumed to be preferable to the corporate-dominated, vulgar twentieth century. Likewise, *Will Penny* (1968) and *Wild Rovers* (1971) discounted the premise of *The Misfits* and *Lonely Are the Brave* that the cowboy had ever been a happy, free individualist or had ever played a meaningful role in frontier progress. Charlton Heston in *Will Penny* and William Holden in *Wild Rovers* are aging cowboys who are saddened by the realization that they have wasted their best years with nothing to show for the daily grind of cowpunching. What little they have earned they have squandered on a Saturday night. It is too late for them to change their lives, which, in the case of *Will Penny*, means that he must refuse the romantic overtures of the young woman he loves, knowing that he can never change into the responsible husband she deserves. As the cowboy in *Wild Rovers*, William Holden attempts to realize his dream of a quiet retirement south of the border by robbing a bank; but he is hunted down and killed by the sons of his employer. His boss (Karl Malden), once a fellow rider who has become a successful rancher and a ruthless, insensitive exemplar of business virtues, must destroy him to discourage other employees from stepping out of line.

Delmer Daves, in *Cowboy* (1958) and *3:10 to Yuma* (1957), questioned aspects of the cowboy myth and stressed the unglamorous life of the small rancher. Yet these films deal with self-employed individuals who in the end realize some reward for their efforts. *Will Penny* and *Wild Rovers* to the contrary show the cowboy as a lowly wage earner, for whom freedom and success were equally remote.

With the exception of *Will Penny* and *Wild Rovers,* Westerns of the late sixties and early seventies follow the precedents of *The Misfits, Lonely Are the Brave,* and *Hud* in contrasting the cowboy's individualism with the collective blandness of the modern age that has made the cowboy obsolescent. The cowboy in *Monte Walsh* (1970) is a sad figure, not because of the hardships of his occupation (as in *Will Penny* and *Wild Rovers*), but because his free and dignified way of life is rapidly fading. In *J. W. Coop* (1971), Peckinpah's *Junior Bonner* (1972), and *The Honkers* (1972), the modern-day cowboy desperately clings to the shoddy rodeo circuit as the only remaining outlet for the rough and tumble cowboy life.[12] Aging cowboys and former rough riders in *Bite the Bullet* (1975) compete in a grueling cross-country horse

[12] Nicholas Ray directed a less than glamorous picture of rodeo life in *The Lusty Men* (1952).

race to retrieve the sense of dignity that has faded with changing times. The risk of life and limb for so little reward is a high but necessary price to pay for refusing to submit to the stale confines of modern society.

The fading importance of the cowboy also characterizes *The Rare Breed* (1966) and *The Cowboys* (1972), although with less despair about the problems of adjusting to modern times. In *The Rare Breed* James Stewart finds compensation in Maureen O'Hara and a prize bull; while in *The Cowboys* the young drovers presumably inherit the rugged virtues of their aged cowboy mentor (John Wayne).[13]

A major contribution to the late sixties' attack on America's frontier heritage and the introduction of a new kind of western hero came from Italy, chiefly from director Sergio Leone. The shortage of Hollywood Westerns on the European market encouraged European productions, especially in Germany and Italy. Some of the German features reached the American screen during the sixties but without much impact or notoriety. They were unimaginative, stiffly acted rehashes of Hollywood themes and featured Hollywood veterans like Lex Barker and Stewart Granger. In 1967, however, United Artists struck gold at the box office with the release of Leone's three Westerns starring Clint Eastwood, the little-known costar of television's *Rawhide* series.

Leone filmed his Westerns in Spain, using a harsh desert landscape to suggest an ominous, parched environment for his fron-

[13] The sad theme of obsolete cowboys reached television in an episode of "Gunsmoke" where Marshal Dillon must track down three cowboys who ran afoul of the law; they cannot find work in changing times that hold few prospects for cowboy work. CBS, "Gunsmoke," 7 October 1974. Movies made for television tend to resemble themes and perspectives of theatrical films. Thus, for example, the *Over-the-Hill Gang* (1969) and *The Over-the-Hill Gang Rides Again* (1970) are comic variations of Peckinpah's vision of anachronistic westerners; these films allude to the sad problem of old-timers who lack a function in changing times. *Mrs. Sundance* (1974) obviously capitalized on the popularity of *Butch Cassidy and the Sundance Kid* (1969) to include a juxtaposition of the freedom and dignity of the frontier outlaw with an empty and materialistic society. Reservations about the value of modern society were not, therefore, peculiar to theatrical movies with their declining audiences, but were also incorporated into television programming that addressed a larger audience of viewers.

tier of human deprivation and depravity where only the fast gun survives. Human decency and morality have no place in this dog-eat-dog world, where the greedy and power-hungry contend for material spoils. Given this cynical notion of the American frontier, material success and sheer survival become the only viable goals for a hero. In a period when most Westerns critical of frontier life involved failures or victims as the major character, the Eastwood hero was indeed unique. In all three films, Eastwood plays a tough, laconic fortune hunter, an almost inhuman part of the arid landscape, devoid of ideals or any purpose save survival and a quick buck. He is heroic only in the sense of recognizing the cutthroat world around him and exercising the guile and skill with a gun to come out on top.

In *A Fistful of Dollars* (1967), Eastwood drifts into the midst of a factional war for control of a town. Without caring about the rights and wrongs of the conflict, he bargains with both sides to kill their respective enemies. His actions are fitting, because the conflict involves only profit and power. The hapless townspeople are the victims whoever wins.

Eastwood again kills for money in *For a Few Dollars More* (1967), this time as a bounty hunter. The film's foreword reads: "Where life had no value, death sometimes had its price." Leone highlights Eastwood's cool, human insensitivity by contrasting him with an older bounty hunter, played by Lee Van Cleef, another heretofore unknown American western actor to become famous via the Via Venito. Van Cleef has suffered a family tragedy and seeks revenge against the same villain Eastwood wants for reward. Van Cleef's character possesses an emotional dimension totally lacking in Eastwood. In Leone's frontier, suffering a loss seems the only source and manifestation of human sensitivity.[14]

In *The Good, the Bad, and the Ugly* (1967), Eastwood competes with two other fortune hunters during the Civil War to retrieve a stolen Army payroll. Leone juxtaposes these violent individuals fighting among themselves for money against the

---

[14] Lee Van Cleef assumed Eastwood's nonchalance in *Sabata* (1970); but in *Death Rides a Horse* (1969), he again displayed a human sensitivity that comes with age—in contrast with the brashness of a younger character.

*The Good, the Bad, and the Ugly* (United Artists, 1967). Personal greed amid the ruins of war.

large-scale slaughter incurred by national rivalries. To kill for money is rational and less destructive than to fight a war for some idealistic cause. Eastwood and his foes spend as much energy eluding the destructive path of the war as they do getting the drop on each other. The film ends with the three contenders facing one another in a final showdown in the center of a vast cemetery of war victims, which also happens to be the burial spot for the payroll.

Leone's next Western, *Once Upon a Time in the West* (1969), differs significantly from both his Eastwood films and the socially critical and pessimistic tone of other Westerns at the time. It still has Leone's usual violent and cruel frontier, but its hero's actions also have moral and social purpose, in contrast with the cynical materialism of Eastwood. The story is episodic and explicitly related to the mythical-historical pageant of the settling of the American frontier. Leone's version of the coming of civilization to the West corresponds in part with other Westerns of the period in that big business corrupts the civilizing process. But Leone concludes his film with the forces of good defeating the moneyed interests. The hero avenges the death of his father, while Claudia Cardinale is left behind in control of the watering spot that will sustain the railroad and the flowering of civilization. Despite stylistic similarities with his previous Westerns—most notably the hero's brutal efficiency and the pervasive cruelties of frontier life—*Once Upon a Time in the West* revived a classic vision that would be seldom repeated in subsequent Westerns.

While *Once Upon a Time in the West* was failing to attract the large audience that had paid for Leone's Eastwood Westerns, Eastwood himself was securing stardom in American films with his tough-loner role. His one departure from the type, Paramount's expensive musical-Western bust, *Paint Your Wagon* (1969), proved disastrous. Don Siegel's *Two Mules for Sister Sara* (1970), with Eastwood playing a cynical fortune hunter who lived only to kill and profit, most closely resembles the three Leone Westerns. The film even sports a lively musical score by Ennio Morricone that is similar to his work for Leone.

In his other American Westerns, Eastwood's tough individualism became a more clearly defined reaction against some form of social injustice that usually implicated a misguided or corrupt legal system. As a deputy sheriff in *Hang 'Em High* (1968) and *Coogan's Bluff* (1969)—the latter a modern urban-crime drama with western elements—Eastwood's tough but fair-minded law enforcement conflicts with an official justice system that is either excessively cruel (*Hang 'Em High*) or distorted by naïvely liberal and bureaucratic considerations (*Coogan's Bluff*). Eastwood is able to bridge, if not correct, the gap between society's legal institutions and true justice.

As *Joe Kidd* (1972) and as the mysterious gunman in *High Plains Drifter* (1973), Eastwood corrects injustice from outside a legal-societal framework that has been thoroughly corrupted by private economic interests. The showdown between Joe Kidd and a vicious landowner symbolically ends in the town courtroom, where Kidd sits in the judge's seat with a pistol aimed at the villain. As the only arbiter of justice in this corrupt community, Joe Kidd gladly pulls the trigger.

Because "good" citizens have allowed their marshal to be brutally murdered, Eastwood, in *High Plains Drifter,* contrives the destruction of an entire town. Moreover, the civic leaders had wanted the marshal removed, because he had discovered that the local mining company—whose interests are identified with the progress of the entire community—was illegally operating on government land. Screenwriter Ernest Tidyman reportedly fashioned the story after the Kitty Genovese incident in New York City, in which an entire neighborhood had looked the other way while a girl was being murdered.[15] Clint Eastwood believed that the film resembled *High Noon* as a commentary on contemporary society's fear of getting involved.[16] Yet, by treating cowardice and complacency in terms of an insensitized, corporate-dominated middle class, the film itself has a more distinctly antiestablishment flavor. The identification of communal progress with the mining company's concern for profit has the timely ring of New Left criticism of America's marketplace mentality.

[15] Arthur C. Knight, interview with Clint Eastwood, 15 March 1973, Special Collections, Doheny Library, University of Southern California, Los Angeles.
[16] Stuart M. Kaminsky, *Clint Eastwood* (New York: Signet Books, 1974), p. 122.

To acknowledge leftist elements in films such as *Joe Kidd* and *High Plains Drifter* is not to deny the reactionary law-and-order implications that have disturbed liberal movie critics, especially in the wake of Eastwood's cop epic *Dirty Harry* (1970). However one labels the Eastwood appeal, it did reflect an overwhelmingly cynical, derogatory view of American society. Eastwood shared with John Wayne the image of a triumphant winner at a time when Westerns tended to condemn society's destructive impact on more fallible central characters.[17] Yet Wayne's victory usually spelled some hope for the preservation of traditional frontier values in spite of the certain, undesirable accompaniments to civilization. Eastwood's Westerns became every bit as despairing as the tragic variety with respect to their vision of an irreparably depraved social order. He may avenge, punish, or merely survive, but without the assurance that his triumph is socially meaningful.

Eastwood's cynical posture also has a comical aspect—most fully realized in the Leone Westerns—that characterizes the heroes of several western comedies of the period (*Waterhole #3* [1967], *Sam Whiskey* [1969], *Dirty Dingus Magee* [1970], and *The Duchess and the Dirtwater Fox* [1976]). The premise of these satirical stabs at the classical Western is that frontier society is basically violent, greedy, and hypocritical, which in turn renders the hero's deviousness a perfectly logical response.[18] After James Coburn, in *Waterhole #3,* wins a showdown by shooting his opponent in the back with a rifle or rapes the crooked sheriff's daughter, a voice off-screen sings tauntingly about the code of the West. On a slightly more serious level, *There Was a Crooked Man* (1970) focuses on a conflict of values between an amiable—but ultimately dangerous—thief and a devoted civil servant. By the end of the film, the civil servant recognizes the

[17] Aside from Westerns described in the text concerning the dehumanizing or destructive impact of social forces on the individual, see: *A Gunfight* (1971); *Lawman* (1971); *The Hunting Party* (1971); *The Man Who Loved Cat Dancing* (1973); *The Deadly Trackers* (1973).

[18] One film of the 1950s that is comparably cynical is Raoul Walsh's *The King and Four Queens* (1956); without the usual last minute hint of social redemption, Walsh details the scheme of a shrewd thief (Clark Gable) to steal some loot from the mother and widows of members of an outlaw gang.

unworthiness of society and its system of justice and rides off with the thief's loot.

Other western parodies, such as *Cat Ballou* (1965), *The Good Guys and the Bad Guys* (1969), and *The Great Scout and Cathouse Thursday* (1976), convey a jaundiced view of society with a gentler, and even sentimental, touch. Robert Mitchum's loss of status and respect as sheriff of an increasingly modern frontier town makes *The Good Guys and the Bad Guys* a comic variation of Peckinpah's *Ride the High Country*. The tearful disappointment of Catherine Ballou (Jane Fonda) at seeing how decrepit the Butch Cassidy gang has become registers the kind of melancholy that Peckinpah brings to his more somber treatment of the nonconforming but nearly extinct outlaw. The underlying pathos of Lee Marvin's over-the-hill gunfighter in *Cat Ballou* comes to the surface in the otherwise farcical *The Great Scout and Cathouse Thursday*. Once again Marvin is a frontier antiquity in a changing West, but he is considerably more pathetic in being denied one last heroic encounter. When he challenges his opponent to a gunfight, the latter tells him to go away before he's turned into dog meat: "It's too late. You're too slow. So am I."

Western parodies are not unique to the 1960s. The formula was subjected to jest by such Hollywood comics as the Marx brothers (*Go West* [1940]), W. C. Fields and Mae West (*My Little Chickadee* [1940]), Bob Hope (*Paleface* [1948]), and Dean Martin and Jerry Lewis (*Pardners* [1956]). Before the sixties, however, the assumptions of a good society, national progress, and the triumph of a law-abiding hero were never seriously questioned in western comedy.

With the appearance of *Blazing Saddles* (1974), even the socially critical Western of the fifties was lampooned. The scene of hypocritical and selfish townspeople meeting in the church was straight out of *High Noon,* while Gene Wilder satirized the alienated gunfighter who in fifties Westerns had suggested the psychologically precarious and unfulfilling nature of life in modern America. Even with its sixties' style of posing an exploited minority hero against a weak society dominated by a corrupt

railroad magnate, *Blazing Saddles* lacked the underlying serious-
ness of *Cat Ballou* or *The Good Guys and the Bad Guys.*

By the mid-seventies, Westerns, such as *Posse* (1975), a
cynical variation on the Watergate-Nixon affair, and *Missouri
Breaks* (1976), still had an antiestablishment flavor; but there
are indications that the abrasive cynicism and despair of the late
sixties and early seventies had run its course. The outlaw-hero
of *Missouri Breaks* defeats the cattle-baron authority figure; and,
like the traditional Westerner, he discovers true love and the joys
of working the land. In *The Outlaw Josey Wales* (1976), Clint
Eastwood departs from the cynical mold he fashioned earlier and
finds solace in a wholesome pioneer community. Charles Bronson,
who along with Eastwood popularized the tough, antisocial hero,
plays a federal agent battling old-fashioned crooks and Indians
in *Breakheart Pass* (1975).

Even thirty years earlier, *Comes a Horseman* (1978) would
have seemed romantic and old-fashioned for a feature Western.
The film's 1940s setting in no way alters its classic premise of
decent ranchers triumphing over a villainous cattle baron. Corporate connivery hovers in the background, but the story of an
honest cowboy who helps the heroine save her ranch brings to
mind the traditional formulaic horse opera.

Sergio Leone, who in *Once Upon a Time in the West* (1969)
presented a more optimistic interpretation of the frontier than
he had in his Eastwood Westerns, produced still another hopeful
vision of the legendary West in *My Name Is Nobody* (1974).
While burlesquing some of the familiar demonstrativeness associated with a Westerner's handling of violence, the film exudes
a genuine affection for the myth of the heroic individual. It
offers some reassurance that the myth will live on, when at the
end of the film the young Terence Hill finds himself out-drawing
his opponents as the retired lawman become legend (Henry
Fonda) had done at the film's beginning.

Whether the legendary, violent loner would or should remain
a part of the American experience is left more open to question
in *The Shootist* (1976). The gunfighter hero (John Wayne) is
killed, but the film suggests that his violent ways—if not his

heroic qualities—are perhaps best left in the past. This point is brought home when a boy admirer avenges the gunfighter's death but quickly discards the gun and joins his mother to take up a way of life his hero had respected but had been ill-equipped to live.

The melancholy demise of the frontier individualist in *The Shootist* recalls to mind *Shane, Ride the High Country,* and many other Westerns. Opening with clips from previous Wayne Westerns, the film has the added appearance of an obituary on the Western itself. The absence of Westerns in the two years since 1976 indeed raises doubts about the future of Hollywood's most durable formula.[19] Yet *The Shootist* is only one among several feature Westerns (*Buffalo Bill and the Indians, The Duchess and the Dirtwater Fox, From Noon till Three, Great Scout and Cathouse Thursday, Missouri Breaks, The Outlaw Josie Wales, The Return of a Man Called Horse*) to emerge two years after Pauline Kael pronounced "The Western is dead." Perhaps this judgment was premature.

There is no demonstrable reason why the Western should be less appropriate for today's audiences than it was for those of yesterday. From World War II through the troubled Cold War years, the Western accommodated a variety of issues and ideas that echoed feelings of confidence and commitment, as well as alienation and disillusionment. Its proved capacity for redefining America's mythic heritage in contemporary terms would suggest, even during the current period of its quiescence, that the Western is an unlikely candidate for cultural oblivion.

[19] As of this writing, *Grayeagle* (1977), *The White Buffalo* (1977), *Comes a Horseman* (1978), and *Goin' South* (1978) are the only Westerns released by a major studio since 1976. All three reflect a mellowing of the severe social criticism that had become commonplace in Westerns during the years of the Vietnam War and Watergate.

## Films

The following list includes all western motion pictures, except for all but the five most pertinent Roy Rogers Westerns,* viewed for this study. Although the research focuses on Westerns since 1945, the list begins with Westerns in 1939 that serve as introductory material. The principal sources for these films are the Library of Congress and television. A few films were viewed in theaters or were rented. Unless otherwise indicated, all films were produced for and released to theaters.

Films that were unavailable, for which plot summaries (continuities, periodical reviews, and pressbooks) were used, are not included unless they are mentioned in the text or notes. The few films listed but not viewed appear with an asterisk (*).

Films are arranged according to year of release, with films released the same year listed alphabetically. Each film listing gives the year of release, title, director, and studio. Studio names are abbreviated as follows:

| | |
|---|---|
| Columbia | COL |
| Metro Goldwyn Mayer | MGM |
| Paramount | PARA |
| Republic | REP |
| RKO Radio | RKO |
| Twentieth Century Fox | FOX |
| United Artists | UA |
| Universal | UNIV |
| Warner Brothers | WB |

* These Roy Rogers films were viewed on television along with thirty-three of his other films produced by Republic between 1938 and 1951.

1939:   *Days of Jesse James*. Joseph Kane. REP.
         *Dodge City*. Michael Curtiz. WB.
         *Drums Along the Mohawk*. John Ford. FOX.
         *Frontier Marshal*. Allan Dwan. FOX.
         *Geronimo*. Paul H. Sloane. PARA.
         *Jesse James*. Henry King. FOX.
         *The Oklahoma Kid*. Lloyd Bacon. WB.
         *Stagecoach*. John Ford. UA.
         *Wall St. Cowboy*. Joseph Kane. REP.

1940:   *Billy the Kid*. David Miller. MGM.
         *The Border Legion*. Joseph Kane. REP.
         *Dark Command*. Raoul Walsh. REP.
         *The Return of Frank James*. Fritz Lang. FOX.
         *Santa Fe Trail*. Michael Curtiz. WB.
         *Virginia City*. Michael Curtiz. WB.
         *The Westerner*. William Wyler. UA.

1941:   *Bad Men of Missouri*. Ray Enright. WB.
         *Belle Starr*. Irving Cummings. FOX.
         *Honky Tonk*. Jack Conway. MGM.
         *Jesse James at Bay*. Joseph Kane. REP.
         *Texas*. George Marshall. COL.
         *They Died with Their Boots On*. Raoul Walsh. WB.
         *Western Union*. Fritz Lang. FOX.

1942:   *American Empire*. William McGann. UA.
         *The Great Man's Lady*. William Wellman. PARA.
         *In Old California*. William McGann. REP.
         *Valley of the Sun*. George Marshall. RKO

1943:   *The Desperadoes*. Charles Vidor. COL.
         *The Kansan*. George Archainbaud. UA.
         *The Outlaw*. Howard Hughes. UA.
         *The Ox Bow Incident*. William Wellman. FOX.

1944:   *Barbary Coast Gent*. Roy del Ruth. MGM.
         *Buffalo Bill*. William Wellman. FOX.
         *Tall in the Saddle*. Edwin Marin. RKO.

1945:   *Along Came Jones*. Stuart Heisler. RKO.
         *Dakota*. Joseph Kane. REP.
         *San Antonio*. David Butler. WB.

1946:   *Angel and the Badman*. James Edward Grant. REP.
        *Bad Bascomb*. S. Sylvan Simon. MGM.
        *Badman's Territory*. Tim Whelan. RKO.
        *Canyon Passage*. Jacques Tourneur. UNIV.
        *Duel in the Sun*. King Vidor. SELZNICK STUDIO.
        *In Old Sacramento*. Joseph Kane. REP.
        *My Darling Clementine*. John Ford. FOX.
        *The Plainsman and the Lady*. Joseph Kane. REP.
        *The Sea of Grass*. Elia Kazan. MGM.

1947:   *California*. John Farrow. PARA.
        *Cheyenne*. Raoul Walsh. WB.
        *The Fabulous Texan*. Edward Ludwig. REP.
        *Gunfighters*. George Waggner. COL.
        *Pursued*. Raoul Walsh. WB.
        *Ramrod*. Andre de Toth. UA.
        *The Romance of Rosy Ridge*. Roy Rowland. MGM.
        *Trail Street*. Ray Enright. RKO.
        *Wyoming*. Joseph Kane. REP.

1948:   *Blood on the Moon*. Robert Wise. RKO.
        *Fort Apache*. John Ford. RKO.
        *Four Faces West*. Alfred E. Green. UA.
        *Fury at Furnace Creek*. Bruce Humberstone. FOX.
        *The Man from Colorado*. Henry Levin. COL.
        *Northwest Stampede*. Albert S. Rogell. EAGLE LION FILMS.
        *The Paleface*. Norman Z. McLeod. PARA.
        *Rachel and the Stranger*. Norman Foster. RKO.
        *Red River*. Howard Hawks. UA.
        *Return of the Bad Men*. Ray Enright. RKO.
        *Roughshod*. Mark Robson. RKO.
        *Silver River*. Raoul Walsh. WB.
        *Station West*. Sidney Lanfield. RKO.
        *Three Godfathers*. John Ford. MGM.
        *Yellow Sky*. William Wellman. FOX.

1949:   *Brimstone*. Joseph Kane. REP.
        *Colorado Territory*.* Raoul Walsh. WB.
        *The Doolins of Oklahoma*. Gordon Douglas. COL.
        *She Wore a Yellow Ribbon*. John Ford. RKO.
        *South of St. Louis*. Ray Enright. WB.
        *Streets of Laredo*. Leslie Fenton. PARA.
        *Whispering Smith*. Leslie Fenton. PARA.

1950:     *Ambush.* Sam Wood. MGM.
        *The Bells of Coronado.* William Witney. REP.
        *Broken Arrow.* Delmer Daves. FOX.
        *Colt .45.* Edwin Marin. WB.
        *Copper Canyon.* John Farrow. PARA.
        *Dallas.* Stuart Heisler. WB.
        *Devil's Doorway.** Anthony Mann. MGM.
        *The Furies.* Anthony Mann. PARA.
        *The Gunfighter.* Henry King. FOX.
        *The Kid from Texas.* Kurt Neumann. UNIV.
        *Montana.* Ray Enright. WB.
        *The Nevadan.* Gordon Douglas. COL.
        *The Outriders.* Roy Rowland. MGM.
        *Rio Grande.* John Ford. REP.
        *Rock Island Trail.* Joseph Kane. REP.
        *Rocky Mountain.* William Keighley. WB.
        *Stars in My Crown.* Jacques Tourneur. MGM.
        *A Ticket to Tomahawk.* Richard Sale. FOX.
        *Two Flags West.* Robert Wise. FOX.
        *Wagonmaster.* John Ford. RKO.
        *Winchester 73.* Anthony Mann. UNIV.

1951:     *Across the Wide Missouri.* William Wellman. MGM.
        *Al Jennings of Oklahoma.* Ray Nazarro. COL.
        *Along the Great Divide.* Raoul Walsh. WB.
        *Best of the Badmen.* William D. Russell. RKO.
        *Branded.* Rudolph Mate. PARA.
        *Cattle Drive.* Kurt Neumann. UNIV.
        *Cavalry Scout.* Leslie Selander. MONOGRAM.
        *Distant Drums.* Raoul Walsh. WB.
        *Fort Worth.* Edwin L. Marin. WB.
        *Golden Girl.* Lloyd Bacon. FOX.
        *The Great Missouri Raid.* Gordon Douglas. PARA.
        *Kansas Raiders.* Ray Enright. UNIV.
        *The Last Outpost.* Lewis R. Foster. PARA.
        *Little Big Horn.* Charles Marquis Warren. LIPPERT.
        *Man in the Saddle.* Andre de Toth. COL.
        *Only the Valiant.* Gordon Douglas. WB.
        *Rawhide.* Henry Hathaway. FOX.
        *Red Mountain.* William Dieterle. PARA.
        *Santa Fe.* Irving Pichel. COL.
        *The Secret of Convict Lake.* Michael Gordon. FOX.

*Silver City.* Byron Haskin. PARA.
*Vengeance Valley.* Richard Thorpe. MGM.
*Warpath.* Byron Haskin. PARA.

1952:    *The Battle at Apache Pass.\** George Sherman. UNIV.
*Bend of the River.* Anthony Mann. UNIV.
*The Big Sky.* Howard Hawks. RKO.
*Bugles in the Afternoon.* Roy Rowland. WB.
*Carson City.* Andre de Toth. WB.
*Cripple Creek.* Ray Nazarro. COL.
*Flaming Feather.* Ray Enright. PARA.
*The Half-Breed.* Stuart Gilmore. RKO.
*High Noon.* Fred Zinnemann. UA.
*Horizons West.* Budd Boetticher. UNIV.
*Indian Uprising.* Ray Nazarro. COL.
*The Iron Mistress.* Gordon Douglas. WB.
*Lone Star.* Vincent Sherman. MGM.
*The Lusty Men.\** Nicholas Ray. RKO.
*Montana Belle.* Allan Dwan. RKO.
*Montana Territory.* Ray Nazarro. COL.
*The Outcasts of Poker Flat.* Joseph M. Newman. FOX.
*Pony Soldier.* Joseph M. Newman. FOX.
*Rancho Notorious.* Fritz Lang. RKO.
*Return of the Texan.* Delmer Daves. FOX.
*The Savage.* George Marshall. PARA.
*Springfield Rifle.* Andre de Toth. WB.
*The Toughest Man in Arizona.* R. G. Springsteen. REP.
*Viva Zapata.* Elia Kazan. FOX.
*Westward the Women.* William Wellman. MGM.
*The Wild North.* Andrew Marton. MGM.

1953:    *Ambush at Tomahawk Gap.* Fred F. Sears. COL.
*Arrowhead.* Charles Marquis Warren. PARA.
*Calamity Jane.* David Butler. WB.
*The Charge at Feather River.* Gordon Douglas. WB.
*Conquest of Cochise.* William Castle. COL.
*Devil's Canyon.* Alfred Werker. RKO.
*Escape from Fort Bravo.* John Sturges. MGM.
*Fort Ti.* William Castle. COL.
*The Great Sioux Uprising.* Lloyd Bacon. UNIV.
*Gun Fury.* Raoul Walsh. COL.
*Gunsmoke.* Nathan Juran. UNIV.

*Hondo.* John Farrow. WB.
*Jack McCall, Desperado.* Sidney Salkow. COL.
*Jack Slade.* Harold Schuster. ALLIED ARTISTS.
*Last of the Comanches.* Andre de Toth. COL.
*The Last Posse.* Alfred Werker. COL.
*The Lawless Breed.* Raoul Walsh. UNIV.
*The Lone Hand.* George Sherman. UNIV.
*The Man Behind the Gun.* Felix Feist. WB.
*The Naked Spur.* Anthony Mann. MGM.
*The Nebraskan.* Fred F. Sears. COL.
*The Pony Express.* Jerry Hopper. PARA.
*Powder River.* Louis King. FOX.
*San Antone.* Joseph Kane. REP.
*Shane.* George Stevens. PARA.
*The Silver Whip.* Harmon Jones. FOX.
*The Stranger Wore a Gun.* Andre de Toth. COL.
*Thunder Over the Plains.* Andre de Toth. WB.
*Tumbleweed.* Nathan Juran. UNIV.

1954:   *The Americano.* William Castle. RKO.
*Apache.* Robert Aldrich. UA.
*Arrow in the Dust.** Leslie Selander. ALLIED ARTISTS.
*Black Horse Canyon.* Jesse Hibbs. UNIV.
*The Boy from Oklahoma.* Michael Curtiz. WB.
*The Broken Lance.* Edward Dmytryk. FOX.
*Cattle Queen of Montana.* Allan Dwan. RKO.
*The Command.* David Butler. WB.
*Dawn at Socorro.* George Sherman. UNIV.
*Drum Beat.* Delmer Daves. WB.
*Four Guns to the Border.* Richard Carlson. UNIV.
*Garden of Evil.* Henry Hathaway. FOX.
*Johnny Guitar.* Nicholas Ray. REP.
*Jubilee Trail.* Joseph Kane. REP.
*The Law versus Billy the Kid.* William Castle. COL.
*The Lawless Rider.* Yakima Canutt. UA.
*The Lone Gun.* Ray Nazarro. UA.
*Overland Pacific.* Fred F. Sears. UA.
*Passion.* Allan Dwan. RKO.
*The Raid.* Hugo Fregonese. FOX.
*River of No Return.* Otto Preminger. FOX.
*Seven Brides for Seven Brothers.* Stanley Donen. MGM.
*The Siege at Red River.* Rudolph Mate. FOX.

*Sitting Bull.* Sidney Salkow. UA.
*Taza, Son of Cochise.* Douglas Sirk. UNIV.
*Three Hours to Kill.* Alfred Werker. COL.
*Three Young Texans.* Henry Levin. FOX.
*Track of the Cat.* William Wellman. WB.
*Vera Cruz.* Robert Aldrich. UA.
*War Arrow.* George Sherman. UNIV.
*The Yellow Tomahawk.* Lesley Selander. UA.

1955:  *At Gunpoint.* Alfred Werker. ALLIED ARTISTS.
*Bad Day at Black Rock.* John Sturges. MGM.
*Chief Crazy Horse.* George Sherman. UNIV.
*Count Three and Pray.* George Sherman. COL.
*Davy Crockett, King of the Wild Frontier.* Norman Foster.
    BUENA VISTA.
*Destry.* George Marshall. UNIV.
*The Far Country.* Anthony Mann. UNIV.
*Five Guns West.* Roger Corman. AMERICAN RELEASING.
*The Indian Fighter.* Andre de Toth. UA.
*The Last Command.* Frank Lloyd. REP.
*A Lawless Street.* Joseph H. Lewis. COL.
*A Man Alone.* Ray Milland. REP.
*The Man from Laramie.* Anthony Mann. COL.
*Man with the Gun.* Richard Wilson. UA.
*Man without a Star.* King Vidor. UNIV.
*Masterson of Kansas.* William Castle. COL.
*The Road to Denver.* Joseph Kane. REP.
*Run for Cover.* Nicholas Ray. PARA.
*Santa Fe Passage.* William Witney. REP.
*Strange Lady in Town.* Mervyn LeRoy. WB.
*Tall Man Riding.* Lesley Selander. WB.
*The Tall Men.* Raoul Walsh. FOX.
*Ten Wanted Men.* H. Bruce Humberstone. COL.
*Texas Lady.* Tim Whelan. RKO.
*Timberjack.* Joseph Kane. REP.
*Top Gun.* Ray Nazarro. UA.
*The Vanishing American.* Joseph Kane. REP.
*The Violent Men.* Rudolph Mate. COL.
*White Feather.* Robert D. Webb. FOX.

1956:  *Backlash.** John Sturges. UNIV.
*Bandido.* Richard Fleischer. UA.

*The Broken Star*. Leslie Selander. UA.
*The Burning Hills*. Stuart Heisler. WB.
*Comanche*. George Sherman. UA.
*Dakota Incident*. Lewis R. Foster. REP.
*The Fastest Gun Alive*. Russell Rouse. MGM.
*Giant*. George Stevens. WB.
*Johnny Concho*. Don McGuire. UA.
*Jubal*. Delmer Daves. COL.
*The Last Frontier*. Anthony Mann. COL.
*The Last Hunt*. Richard Brooks. MGM.
*The Last Wagon*. Delmer Daves. FOX.
*Love Me Tender*. Robert D. Webb. FOX.
*The Man from Del Rio*. Harry Horner. UA.
*The Maverick Queen*. Joseph Kane. REP.
*Pardners*. Norman Taurog. PARA.
*Pillars in the Sky*. George Marshall. UNIV.
*The Proud Ones*. Robert D. Webb. FOX.
*The Rawhide Years*. Rudolph Mate. UNIV.
*Rebel in Town*. Alfred Werker. UA.
*Red Sundown*. Jack Arnold. UNIV.
*Reprisal*. George Sherman. COL.
*Santiago*. Gordon Douglas. WB.
*The Searchers*. John Ford. WB.
*Showdown at Abilene*. Charles Haas. UNIV.
*Stranger at My Door*. William Witney. REP.
*Tension at Table Rock*. Charles Marquis Warren. RKO.
*Three Violent People*. Rudolph Mate. PARA.
*Tribute to a Bad Man*. Robert Wise. MGM.
*Walk the Proud Land*. Jesse Hibbs. UNIV.
*Westward Ho the Wagons*. William Beudine. BUENA VISTA.

1957:   *Black Patch*. Allen H. Miner. WB.
        *Decision at Sundown*. Budd Boetticher. COL.
        *Drango*. Hall Bartlett and Jules Bricken. UA.
        *Forty Guns*. Samuel Fuller. FOX.
        *Gun Battle at Monterey*. Carl K. Hittelman and Sidney A.
            Franklin, Jr. UA.
        *Gun Glory*. Roy Rowland. MGM.
        *Gunfight at the O.K. Corral*. John Sturges. PARA.
        *The Guns of Fort Petticoat*. George Marshall. COL.
        *Gunsight Ridge*. Francis D. Lyon. UA.
        *The Halliday Brand*. Joseph H. Lewis. UA.

*The Hard Man.* George Sherman. COL.
*The Iron Sheriff.* Sidney Salkow. UA.
*The King and Four Queens.* Raoul Walsh. UA.
*The Lonely Man.* Henry Levin. PARA.
*Night Passage.* James Neilson. UNIV.
*The Quiet Gun.* William Claxton. FOX.
*The Ride Back.* Allen H. Miner. UA.
*Ride Out for Revenge.* Bernard Girard. COL.
*Run of the Arrow.* Samuel Fuller. RKO.
*Shoot-Out at Medicine Bend.* Richard L. Bare. WB.
*The Tall Stranger.* Thomas Carr. ALLIED ARTISTS.
*The Tall T.* Budd Boetticher. COL.
*3:10 to Yuma.* Delmer Daves. COL.
*The Tin Star.* Anthony Mann. PARA.
*Trooper Hook.* Charles Marquis Warren. UA.
*The True Story of Jesse James.* Nicholas Ray. FOX.
*Utah Blaine.* Fred F. Sears. COL.
*Valerie.* Gerd Oswald. UA.

1958:     *Apache Territory.* Ray Nazarro. COL.
*The Badlanders.* Delmer Daves. MGM.
*The Big Country.* William Wyler. UA.
*The Bravados.* Henry King. FOX.
*Buchanan Rides Alone.* Budd Boetticher. COL.
*Canyon River.* Harmon Jones. ALLIED ARTISTS.
*Cattle Empire.* Charles Marquis Warren. FOX.
*Cowboy.* Delmer Daves. COL.
*Day of the Bad Man.* Harry Keller. UNIV.
*The Fiend Who Walked the West.* Gordon Douglas. FOX.
*Fort Dobbs.* Gordon Douglas. WB.
*From Hell to Texas.* Henry Hathaway. FOX.
*Gunman's Walk.* Phil Karlson. COL.
*The Law and Jake Wade.* John Sturges. MGM.
*The Left-Handed Gun.* Arthur Penn. WB.
*Man of the West.* Anthony Mann. UA.
*Ride a Crooked Trail.* Jesse Hibbs. UNIV.
*Saddle the Wind.* Robert Parrish. MGM.
*The Sheepman.* George Marshall. MGM.
*Showdown at Boot Hill.* Gene Fowler, Jr. FOX
*Sierra Baron.* James B. Clark. FOX.
*Tonka.* Lewis R. Foster. BUENA VISTA.
*Wind Across the Everglades.* Nicholas Ray. WB.

1959:   *Curse of the Undead.* Edward Dein. UNIV.
        *Day of the Outlaw.* Andre de Toth. UA.
        *Face of a Fugitive.* Paul Wendkos. COL.
        *Good Day for a Hanging.* Nathan Juran. COL.
        *Gunfight at Dodge City.* Joseph M. Newman. UA.
        *The Hanging Tree.* Delmer Daves. WB.
        *The Hangman.* Michael Curtiz. PARA.
        *The Horse Soldiers.* John Ford. UA.
        *The Jayhawkers.* Melvin Frank. PARA.
        *Last Train from Gun Hill.* John Sturges. PARA.
        *No Name on the Bullet.* Jack Arnold. UNIV.
        *Ride Lonesome.* Budd Boetticher. COL.
        *Rio Bravo.* Howard Hawks. WB.
        *These Thousand Hills.* Richard Fleischer. FOX.
        *Thunder in the Sun.* Russell Rouse. PARA.
        *The Unforgiven.* John Huston. UA.
        *Warlock.* Edward Dmytryk. FOX.
        *Westbound.* Budd Boetticher. WB.
        *The Wild and the Innocent.* Jack Sher. UNIV.
        *The Wonderful Country.* Robert Parrish. UA.
        *Yellowstone Kelly.* Gordon Douglas. WB.

1960:   *The Alamo.* John Wayne. UA.
        *Comanche Station.* Budd Boetticher. COL.
        *Flaming Star.* Donald Siegel. FOX.
        *Guns of the Timberland.* Robert D. Webb. WB.
        *Heller in Pink Tights.* George Cukor. PARA.
        *The Magnificent Seven.* John Sturges. UA.
        *North to Alaska.* Henry Hathaway. FOX.
        *One Foot in Hell.* James B. Clark. FOX.
        *Sergeant Rutledge.* John Ford. WB.
        *A Thunder of Drums.** Joseph M. Newman. MGM.
        *Walk Like a Dragon.* James Clavell. PARA.

1961:   *The Comancheros.* Michael Curtiz. FOX.
        *Gold of the Seven Saints.* Gordon Douglas. WB.
        *The Last Sunset.* Robert Aldrich. UNIV.
        *The Misfits.* John Huston. UA.
        *One Eyed Jacks.* Marlon Brando. PARA.
        *Posse From Hell.* Herbert Coleman. UNIV.
        *Two Rode Together.* John Ford. COL.

1962: *Geronimo.* Arnold Laven. UA.
*How the West Was Won.* John Ford, Henry Hathaway, George Marshall. MGM.
*Lonely Are the Brave.* David Miller. UNIV.
*The Man Who Shot Liberty Valence.* John Ford. PARA.
*Ride the High Country.* Sam Peckinpah. MGM.
*Six Black Horses.* Harry Keller. UNIV.

1963: *Cattle King.* Tay Garnett. MGM.
*Four for Texas.* Robert Aldrich. WB.
*The Gun Hawk.* Edward Ludwig. ALLIED ARTISTS.
*Hud.* Martin Ritt. PARA.
*McLintock.* Andrew V. McLaglen. UA.
*Showdown.* R. G. Springsteen. UNIV.

1964: *Bullet for a Badman.* R. G. Springsteen. UNIV.
*Cheyenne Autumn.* John Ford. WB.
*Circus World.* Henry Hathaway. UA.
*A Distant Trumpet.* Raoul Walsh. WB.
*He Rides Tall.* R. G. Springsteen. UNIV.
*Invitation to a Gunfighter.* Richard Wilson. UA.
*Mail Order Bride.* Burt Kennedy. MGM.
*The Quick Gun.* Sidney Salkow. COL.
*Rio Conchos.* Gordon Douglas. FOX.

1965: *The Bounty Killer.* Spencer G. Bennet. EMBASSY.
*Cat Ballou.* Elliot Silverstein. COL.
*The Glory Guys.* Arnold Laven. UA.
*The Great Sioux Massacre.* Sidney Salkow. COL.
*The Hallelujah Trail.* John Sturges. UA.
*Major Dundee.* Sam Peckinpah. COL.
*Requiem for a Gunfighter.* Spencer G. Bennet. EMBASSY.
*The Rounders.* Burt Kennedy. MGM.
*Shenandoah.* Andrew V. McLaglen. UNIV.
*The Sons of Katie Elder.* Henry Hathaway. PARA.
*Taggart.* R. G. Springsteen. UNIV.

1966: *Alvarez Kelly.* Edward Dmytryk. COL.
*The Appaloosa.* Sidney J. Furie. UNIV.
*A Big Hand for the Little Lady.* Fielder Cook. WB.
*Billy the Kid vs. Dracula.* William Beaudine. EMBASSY.
*Duel at Diablo.* Ralph Nelson. UA.
*Forty Guns to Apache Pass.* William Witney. COL.

*Night of the Grizzly*. Joseph Pevney. PARA.
*The Plainsman*. David Lowell Rich. UNIV.
*The Professionals*. Richard Brooks. COL.
*The Rare Breed*. Andrew V. McLaglen. UNIV.
*Return of the Seven*. Burt Kennedy. UA.
*Ride Beyond Vengeance*. Bernard McEveety. COL.
*Stagecoach*. Gordon Douglas. FOX.
*Texas Across the River*. Michael Gordon. UNIV.

1967:   *Custer of the West*. Robert Siodmak. CINERAMA.
*El Dorado*. Howard Hawks. PARA.
*A Fistful of Dollars*. Sergio Leone. UA.
*For a Few Dollars More*. Sergio Leone. UA.
*The Good, the Bad, and the Ugly*. Sergio Leone. UA.
*Gunfight in Abilene*. William Hale. UNIV.
*Hombre*. Martin Ritt. FOX.
*Hour of the Gun*. John Sturges. UA.
*The Last Challenge*. Richard Thorpe. MGM.
*The Ride to Hangman's Tree*. Alan Rafkin. UNIV.
*Rough Night in Jericho*. Arnold Lavin. UNIV.
*The War Wagon*. Burt Kennedy. UNIV.
*Waterhole #3*. William D. Graham. PARA.
*The Way West*. Andrew V. McLaglen. UA.
*Welcome to Hard Times*. Burt Kennedy. MGM.

1968:   *The Ballad of Josie*. Andrew V. McLaglen. UNIV.
*Bandolero*. Andrew V. McLaglen. FOX.
*Blue*. Silvio Narizzano. PARA.
*Coogan's Bluff*. Donald Siegel. UNIV.
*Day of the Evil Gun*. Jerry Thorpe. MGM.
*Firecreek*. Vincent McEveety. WB.
*Five Card Stud*. Henry Hathaway. PARA.
*Guns for San Sebastian*. Henri Verneuil. MGM.
*Hang 'Em High*. Ted Post. UA.
*The Scalphunters*. Sydney Pollack. UA.
*Villa Rides*. Buzz Kulik. PARA.
*Will Penny*. Tom Gries. PARA.

1969:   *Butch Cassidy and the Sundance Kid*. George Roy Hill.
FOX.
*Charro*. Charles Marquis Warren. NATIONAL GENERAL.
*Death of a Gunfighter*. Allen Smithee. UNIV.
*Death Rides a Horse*. Giulio Petroni. UA.

*The Desperados*. Henry Levin. COL.
*The Good Guys and the Bad Guys*. Burt Kennedy. WB.
*Heaven with a Gun*. Lee H. Katzin. MGM.
*Mackenna's Gold*. J. Lee Thompson. COL.
*A Man Called Gannon*. James Goldstone. UNIV.
*Once Upon a Time in the West*. Sergio Leone. PARA.
*100 Rifles*. Tom Gries. FOX.
*Sam Whiskey*. Arnold Laven. UA.
*The Stalking Moon*. Robert Mulligan. NATIONAL GENERAL.
*Support Your Local Sheriff*. Burt Kennedy. UA.
*True Grit*. Henry Hathaway. PARA.
*The Undefeated*. Andrew V. McLaglen. FOX.
*The Wild Bunch*. Sam Peckinpah. WB.

1970: *The Ballad of Cable Hogue*. Sam Peckinpah. WB.
*Barquero*. Gordon Douglas. UA.
*The Cheyenne Social Club*. Gene Kelly. NATIONAL GEN-
ERAL.
*Chisum*. Andrew V. McLaglen. WB.
*The Deserter*. Burt Kennedy. PARA.
*Dirty Dingus Magee*. Burt Kennedy. MGM.
*El Condor*. John Guillermin. NATIONAL GENERAL.
*Little Big Man*. Arthur Penn. NATIONAL GENERAL.
*Macho Callahan*. Bernard Kowalski. AVCO-EMBASSY.
*A Man Called Horse*. Elliot Silverstein. NATIONAL GEN-
ERAL.
*Monte Walsh*. William A. Fraker. NATIONAL GENERAL.
*Rio Lobo*. Howard Hawks. NATIONAL GENERAL.
*Sabata*. Frank Kramer. UA.
*Soldier Blue*. Ralph Nelson. AVCO-EMBASSY.
*Tell Them Willie Boy Is Here*. Abraham Polonsky. UNIV.
*There Was a Crooked Man*. Joseph Mankiewicz. WB.
*Two Mules for Sister Sara*. Donald Siegel. UNIV.
*Young Billy Young*. Burt Kennedy. UA.

1971: *Big Jake*. George Sherman. NATIONAL GENERAL.
*Catlow*. Sam Wannamaker. MGM.
*Doc*. Frank Perry. UA.
*A Gunfight*. Lamont Johnson. PARA.
*The Hired Hand*. Peter Fonda. UNIV.
*The Hunting Party*.* Don Medford. UA.
*Lawman*. Michael Winner. UA.
*A Man Called Sledge*. Vic Morrow. COL.

*McCabe and Mrs. Miller.* Robert Altman. WB.
*One More Train to Rob.* Andrew V. McLaglen. UNIV.
*Red Sun.* Terence Young. NATIONAL GENERAL.
*Shoot Out.* Henry Hathaway. UNIV.
*Skin Game.* Paul Bogart. WB.
*Something Big.* Andrew V. McLaglen. NATIONAL GEN-
    ERAL.
*Support Your Local Gunfighter.* Burt Kennedy. UA.
*Valdez Is Coming.* Edwin Sherin. UA.
*Wild Rovers.* Blake Edwards. MGM.

1972:   *Bad Company.* Robert Benton. PARA.
        *Buck and the Preacher.* Sidney Poitier. COL.
        *Chato's Land.* Michael Winner. UA.
        *The Cowboys.* Mark Rydell. WB.
        *The Culpepper Cattle Co.* Dick Richards. FOX.
        *The Great Northfield Minnesota Raid.* Philip Kaufman.
            UNIV.
        *Hannie Caulder.* Burt Kennedy. PARA.
        *The Honkers.* Steve Ihnat. UA.
        *J. W. Coop.* Cliff Robertson. COL.
        *Jeremiah Johnson.* Sydney Pollack. WB.
        *Junior Bonner.* Sam Peckinpah. CINERAMA.
        *The Life and Times of Judge Roy Bean.* John Huston.
            FOX.
        *Soul Soldier.* John Cardos. FANFARE.
        *They Call Me Trinity.* E. B. Clucher. AVCO-EMBASSY.
        *The Train Robbers.* Burt Kennedy. WB.
        *Ulzana's Raid.* Robert Aldrich. UNIV.
        *When the Legends Die.* Stuart Millar. FOX.

1973:   *Cahill: United States Marshal.* Andrew V. McLaglen. WB.
        *The Deadly Trackers.* Barry Shear. WB.
        *Dirty Little Billy.* Stan Dragoti. COL.
        *High Plains Drifter.* Clint Eastwood. UNIV.
        *The Man Who Loved Cat Dancing.* Richard C. Sarafian.
            MGM.
        *Pat Garrett and Billy the Kid.* Sam Peckinpah. MGM.
        *Santee.* Gary Nelson. CROWN INTERNATIONAL.
        *Showdown.* George Seaton. UNIV.

1974:   *Blazing Saddles.* Mel Brooks. WB.
        *The Castaway Cowboy.* Vincent McEveety. BUENA VISTA.
        *My Name Is Nobody.* Tinino Valerii. UNIV.

*The Spikes Gang.* Richard Fleischer. UA.

1975: *Against a Crooked Sky.* Earl Bellamy. DOTY-DAYTON.
*Bite the Bullet.* Richard Brooks. COL.
*Breakheart Pass.* Tom Gries. UA.
*Hearts of the West.* Howard Zieff. MGM.
*Posse.* Kirk Douglas. PARA.
*Rooster Cogburn.* Stuart Millar. UNIV.

1976: *Buffalo Bill and the Indians: Or Sitting Bull's History
Lesson.* Robert Altman. UA.
*The Duchess and the Dirtwater Fox.* Melvin Frank. FOX.
*From Noon till 3.* Frank Gilroy. UA.
*Great Scout and Cathouse Thursday.* Don Taylor. AMERI-
CAN INTERNATIONAL.
*Missouri Breaks.* Arthur Penn. UA.
*The Outlaw Josey Wales.* Clint Eastwood. WB.
*The Return of a Man Called Horse.* Irvin Kershner. UA.
*The Shootist.* Don Siegel. PARA.

1977: *Grayeagle.* Charles B. Pierce. AMERICAN INTERNATIONAL.
*The White Buffalo.* J. Lee Thompson. UA.

1978: *Comes a Horseman.* Alan Pakula. UA.
*Goin' South.* Jack Nicholson. PARA.

## Guides and Bibliographies

Adams, Les, and Buck Rainey. *Shoot-Em-Ups: The Complete Refer-
ence Guide to Westerns of the Sound Era.* New Rochelle, N.Y.:
Arlington House, 1978.
Batty, Linda. *Retrospective Index to Film Periodicals, 1930–1971.*
New York: Xerox Education Co., 1975.
Bukalski, Peter J., comp. *Film Research: A Critical Bibliography
with Annotations and Essay.* Boston: G. K. Hall & Co., 1972.
*Catalogue of Copyright Entries, Cumulative Series, Motion Pictures,
1912–1969.* 4 vols. Washington, D.C.: U.S. Copyright Office, 1971.
Cronon, E. David, and Theodore D. Rosenof, comps. *The Second
World War and the Atomic Age, 1940–1973.* Northbrook, Ill.:
AHM Publishing Co., 1975.
Eyles, Allen. *The Western.* New York: A. S. Barnes & Co., 1975.
Limbacher, James L., comp. *Remakes, Series and Sequels on Film
and Television.* Dearborn, Mich.: Dearborn Public Library, 1969.
Manchel, Frank. *Film Study: A Resource Guide.* Rutherford, N.J.:
Fairleigh Dickinson Univ. Press, 1973.

Mehr, Linda Harris, ed. *Motion Pictures, Television and Radio: A Union Catalogue of Manuscript and Special Collections in the Western United States.* Boston: G. K. Hall & Co., 1977.

Nachbar, Jack. "A Checklist of Published Materials on Western Movies." *Journal of Popular Film* 2 (Fall 1973):411–28.

Nachbar, John G. *Western Films: An Annotated Critical Bibliography.* New York: Garland Publishing, 1975.

*The New York Times Film Reviews, 1913–1968.* 6 vols. Vols. 1–5, reviews; vol. 6, appendix and index. Supplements (1969–70, 1971–72, 1973–74). New York: New York Times and Arno Press, 1970–.

Parish, James Robert, and Michael R. Pitts. *Film Directors: A Guide to Their American Films.* Metuchen, N.J.: Scarecrow Press, 1974.

———. *The Great Western Pictures.* Metuchen, N.J.: Scarecrow Press, 1976.

Perry, Ted. *Performing Arts Resources, 1974.* New York: Drama Books Specialists, 1975.

Pickard, Roy. *A Companion to the Movies: From 1903 to the Present Day.* London: Lutterworth Press, 1972.

Reilly, Adam, comp. *Current Film Periodicals in English.* Rev. ed. New York: Educational Film Library Assn., 1970.

Schuster, Mel, comp. *Motion Picture Directors: A Bibliography of Magazine and Periodical Articles, 1900–1972.* Metuchen, N.J.: Scarecrow Press, 1973.

———, comp. *Motion Picture Performers: A Bibliography of Magazine and Periodical Articles, 1900–1969.* Metuchen, N.J.: Scarecrow Press, 1971.

Stapleton, Margaret L. *The Truman and Eisenhower Years, 1945–1960: A Selective Bibliography.* Metuchen, N.J.: Scarecrow Press, 1973.

*Who Wrote the Movies and What Else Did He Write.* Los Angeles: Academy of Motion Picture Arts and Sciences and Writers Guild of America, 1970.

Young, William C. *American Theatrical Arts: A Guide to Manuscripts and Special Collections in the United States and Canada.* Chicago: American Library Assn., 1971.

*Unpublished Materials*
SPECIAL COLLECTIONS

Beverly Hills, Calif. American Film Institute. Charles K. Feldman Library. Oral History Collection. Robert Aldrich (transcript), 2 November 1971; Budd Boetticher (transcript), 1 June 1970;

Merian C. Cooper (transcript), 7 May 1972; Henry Hathaway (tape), 18 June 1973; Howard Hawks (transcript), 19 November 1970; Joel McCrea (tape), 2 August 1971; Ralph Nelson (transcript), 1 November 1972; Martin Ritt (transcript), 4 May 1970; Raoul Walsh (transcript), 16 February 1972; John Wayne (tape), 6 July 1971.

Los Angeles, Calif. Academy of Motion Picture Arts and Sciences. Margaret Herrick Library. Clipping files, articles from magazines and newspapers, includes biography files on filmmakers (stars, directors, producers) and genre files, including the Western.

Los Angeles, Calif. University of California at Los Angeles. Research Library. Department of Special Collections. Ralph Nelson Papers: boxes 29–32 (*"Duel at Diablo"*) and boxes 55–59 (*"Soldier Blue"*). Stanley Kramer Papers: box 6 (*"High Noon"*) and boxes 70–72 (*"Invitation to a Gunfighter"*).

Los Angeles, California. University of Southern California. Doheny Library. Arthur Knight and USC cinema students, interviews (tapes): Clint Eastwood, 15 March 1973; Glenn Ford, 30 November 1967; Carl Foreman, 2 January 1964; Tom Gries, 22 October 1970; Lamont Johnson, 20 May 1971; Martin Rackin, 26 May 1966; Mark Rydell, Spring 1972; John Sturges, 9 May 1963. Michael Hoey, interview of Stanley Kramer, 30 October 1973.

Washington, D.C. Library of Congress. Motion Picture Division. Continuities (scripts based on final film) and pressbooks.

PERSONAL INTERVIEWS

Daves, Delmer, June 1973. Beverly Hills, Calif.
Douglas, Gordon. June 1973. Hollywood, Calif.
Kane, Joseph. June 1973. Pacific Palisades, Calif.
Marshall, George. June 1973. Hollywood, Calif.
Miller, Winston. June 1973. Beverly Hills, Calif.
Rosenberg, Aaron, June 1973. Beverly Hills, Calif.
Webb, James R. June 1973. Beverly Hills, Calif.
Wilson, Richard and Elizabeth. June 1973. Santa Monica, Calif.

*Books and Articles*
THE WESTERN*

Bazin, Andre. *What is Cinema?* Translated by Hugh Gray. Vol. 2. Berkeley: University of California Press, 1971.

* Includes studies of filmmakers commonly associated with the Western; also studies that contain an essay or chapter on the Western.

Bogdanovich, Peter. *John Ford*. Highgate Hill, London: Studio Vista, 1967.

Brauer, Ralph and Donna. *The Horse, the Gun and the Piece of Property: Changing Images of the TV Western*. Bowling Green, O.: Bowling Green University Press, 1975.

Canham, Kingsley. *The Hollywood Professionals: Michael Curtiz, Raoul Walsh, Henry Hathaway*. Vol. 1. New York: A. S. Barnes & Co., 1973.

Caulder, Jennie. *There Must Be a Long Ranger: The American West in Film and Reality*. New York: Taplinger Publishing Co., 1975.

Cawelti, John. *The Six-Gun Mystique*. Bowling Green, O.: Bowling Green University Popular Press, 1971.

Clapham, Walter C. *Western Movies*. London: Octopus Books, 1974.

Davis, David Brion. "Ten-Gallon Hero." *The National Temper*. Edited by Lawrence W. Levine and Robert Middlebauff. New York: Harcourt, Brace & World, 1968.

Everson, William K. *A Pictorial History of the Western Film*. New York: Citadel Press, 1969.

Fenin, George N. "The Western: Old and New." *Film Culture* (May-June 1956):7–10.

————, and Everson, William K. *The Western: From Silents to the Seventies*. New York: Grossman Publishers, 1973.

French, Philip. *Westerns*. New York: Viking Press, 1974.

Friar, Ralph E., and Friar, Natasha A. *The Only Good Indian . . .: The Hollywood Gospel*. New York: Drama Book Specialists, 1972.

Hutton, Paul A. "From Little Big Horn to Little Big Man: The Changing Image of a Western Hero in Popular Culture." *The Western Historical Quarterly* 7 (January 1976):19–45.

Jacobson, Herbert L. "Cowboy, Pioneer and American Soldier." *Sight and Sound* 22 (April-June 1953):189–90.

Kael, Pauline. "The Street Western." *New Yorker,* February 25, 1974, pp. 100–106.

Kaminsky, Stuart M. *Clint Eastwood*. New York: Signet Books, 1974.

Kitses, Jim. *Horizons West*. Bloomington: Indiana University Press, 1969.

Manchel, Frank. *Cameras West*. Englewood Cliffs, N.J.: Prentice Hall, 1971.

Maynard, Richard A., ed. *The American West on Film: Myth and Reality*. Rochelle Park, N.J.: Hayden Book Co., 1974.

McArthur, Colin. "Sam Peckinpah's West." *Sight and Sound* 36 (Autumn 1967):180–83.

McBride, Joseph, ed. *Focus on Howard Hawks.* Englewood Cliffs, N.J.: Prentice-Hall, 1972.

McBride, Joseph, and Wilmington, Michael. "Prisoner of the Desert." *Sight and Sound* 40 (Autumn 1971):210–14.

———. *John Ford.* New York: Da Capo Press, 1975.

McMurtry, Larry. "Cowboys, Movies, Myths, and Cadillacs: Realism in the Western." *Man in the Movies.* Edited by W. R. Robinson. Baltimore: Penguin Books, 1967.

Nachbar, Jack, ed. *Focus on the Western.* Englewood Cliffs, N.J.: Prentice-Hall, 1974.

Parkinson, Michael, and Jeavons, Clyde. *A Pictorial History of Westerns.* London: Hamlyn Publishing Group, 1972.

Pilkington, William T., and Don Graham, eds. *Western Movies.* Albuquerque: University of New Mexico Press, 1979.

Place, J. A. *The Western Films of John Ford.* Secaucus, N.J.: Citadel Press, 1974.

*Playboy.* Interview with John Wayne. May 1971.

———. Interview with Sam Peckinpah. August 1972.

Sarris, Andrew. *The John Ford Movie Mystery.* Bloomington: Indiana University Press, 1975.

Smith, Henry Nash. *The Virgin Land: The American West as Symbol and Myth.* New York: Vintage Books, 1950.

Soloman, Stanley J. *Beyond Formula.* New York: Harcourt Brace Jovanovich, 1976.

Steckmesser, Kent Ladd. *The Western Hero in History and Legend.* Norman: University of Oklahoma Press, 1965.

Tuska, John. *The Filming of the West.* Garden City, N.Y.: Doubleday & Co., 1976.

Warshow, Robert. *The Immediate Experience: Movies, Comics, Theater and Other Aspects of Popular Culture.* New York: Doubleday & Co., 1962.

Whitehall, Richard. "The Heroes Are Tired." *Film Quarterly* 20 (Winter 1966–67):12–24.

———. "Talking with Peckinpah." *Sight and Sound* 38 (Autumn 1969):172–75.

Wood, Robin. *Howard Hawks.* Garden City, New York: Doubleday & Co., 1968.

Wright, Will. *Six Guns and Society: A Structural Study of the Western.* Berkeley: University of California Press, 1975.

Zolotow, Maurice. *Shooting Star: A Biography of John Wayne.* New York: Simon & Schuster, 1974.

## MOVIES AND POPULAR CULTURE

Andrew, J. Dudley. *The Major Film Theories: An Introduction.* New York: Oxford University Press, 1976.

Baxter, John. *Hollywood in the Thirties.* New York: A. S. Barnes, 1968.

———. *Hollywood in the Sixties.* New York: A. S. Barnes, 1972.

Bergman, Andrew. *We're in the Money.* New York: New York University Press, 1971.

Bogle, Donald. *Toms, Coons, Mulattoes, Mammies, and Bucks: An Interpretive History of Blacks in American Films.* New York: Bantam Books, 1974.

Corliss, Richard. *Talking Picture: Screenwriters in the American Cinema, 1927–1973.* Woodstock, N.J.: Overlook Press, 1974.

———, ed. *The Hollywood Screenwriters: A Film Comment Book.* New York: Avon Books, 1972.

Cripps, Thomas. "The Death of Rastus: Negroes in American Films since 1945." *The Movies: An American Idiom.* Edited by Arthur McClure. Rutherford, N.J.: Fairleigh Dickinson University Press, 1971.

Deming, Barbara. *Running Away from Myself: A Dream Portrait of America Drawn from the Films of the Forties.* New York: Grossman Publishers, 1969.

Dowdy, Andrew. *The Films of the Fifties: The American State of Mind.* New York: William Morrow & Co., 1975.

Fell, John L. *Film: An Introduction.* New York: Praeger Publishers, 1975.

Fishwick, Marshall. *The Hero American Style.* New York: David McKay Co., 1969.

Furhammar, Leif, and Isaksson, Folke. *Politics and Films.* New York: Praeger Publishers, 1971.

Gans, Herbert J. *Popular Culture and High Culture: An Analysis and Evalutaion of Taste.* New York: Basic Books, 1974.

Gow, Gordon. *Hollywood in the Fifties.* New York: A. S. Barnes, 1971.

Greenburg, Joel, and Higham, Charles. *Hollywood in the Forties.* New York: Paperback Library, 1970.

Higham, Charles. *Hollywood at Sunset.* New York: Saturday Review Press, 1972.

Houston, Penelope. *The Contemporary Cinema.* London: Penguin Books, 1963.

Jacobs, Lewis. *The Rise of the American Film.* New York: Teachers College Press, 1939.

———. "World War II and the American Film." *The Movies: An American Idiom.* Edited by Arthur McClure. Rutherford, N.J.: Fairleigh Dickinson University Press, 1971.

Jarvie, I. C. *Movies and Society.* New York: Basic Books, 1970.

———. *Movies as Social Criticism: Aspects of Their Social Psychology.* Metuchen, N.J.: Scarecrow Press, 1978.

*Journal of Popular Culture* 9:2 (Fall 1975), pp. 353/1-508/156, and 11 (Summer 1977), pp. 139/1-289/151. [Special sections devoted to theories and methodologies in the study of popular culture.]

Jowett, Garth. *Film: The Democratic Art.* Boston: Little, Brown, 1976.

Kael, Pauline. *I Lost It at the Movies.* New York: Bantam Books, 1966.

———. *Kiss Kiss Bang Bang.* New York: Bantam Books, 1969.

Knight, Arthur. *The Liveliest Art: A Panoramic History of the Movies.* New York: Mentor Book, 1957.

Lowenthal, Leo. *Literature, Popular Culture, and Society.* Palo Alto, Calif.: Pacific Books, 1968.

MacCann, Richard Dyer. *The People's Films: A Political History of U.S. Government Motion Pictures.* New York: Hastings House, 1973.

Mapp, Edward. *Blacks in American Film: Today and Yesterday.* Metuchen, N.J.: Scarecrow Press, 1972.

Mayersburg, Paul. *Hollywood: The Haunted House.* London: Penguin Books, 1967.

McArthur, Colin. *Underworld USA.* New York: Viking Press, 1972.

McConnell, Frank. *The Spoken Seen: Film and the Romantic Imagination.* Baltimore: Johns Hopkins University Press, 1975.

Morella, Joe, and Epstein, Edward Z. *Rebels: The Rebel Hero in Films.* New York: Citadel Press, 1971.

Noble, Peter. *The Negro in Films.* Port Washington, N.Y.: Kennikat Press, 1969.

Nye, Russel, *The Unembarrassed Muse: The Popular Arts in America.* New York: Dial Press, 1970.

O'Connor, John E., and Martin A. Jackson, eds. *American History/American Film: Interpreting the Hollywood Image.* New York: Frederick Ungar, 1979.

Powdermaker, Hortense. *Hollywood: The Dream Factory*. London: Secker & Warburg, 1951.

Reisman, Leon. "Cinema Technique and Mass Culture." *American Quarterly* 1 (1949):314–25.

Robinson, David. *The History of World Cinema*. New York: Stein & Day, 1973.

————. *Hollywood in the Twenties*. New York: A. S. Barnes, 1968.

Sarris, Andrew, ed. *Interviews with Film Directors*. New York: Discus Books, 1969.

Shadoian, Jack. "America the Ugly: Phil Karlson's *99 River Street*." *Film Culture* (Spring 1972), pp. 286–92.

————. *Dreams and Dead Ends: The American Gangster/Crime Film*. Cambridge, Mass.: The M.I.T. Press, 1977.

Sherman, Eric, and Rubin, Martin. *The Director's Event: Interviews with Five American Film-Makers*. New York: Signet Books, 1972.

Sklar, Robert. *Movie-Made America: A Social History of American Movies*. New York: Random House, 1975.

Smith, Julian. *Looking Away: Hollywood and Vietnam*. New York: Charles Scribner's Sons, 1975.

Smith, Paul, ed. *The Historian and Film*. Cambridge: Cambridge University Press, 1976.

Sontag, Susan. *Against Interpretation*. New York: Farrar, Straus, & Giroux, 1966.

White, David Manning, and Richard Averson. *The Celluloid Weapon: Social Comment in the American Film*. Boston: Beacon Press, 1972.

Wood, Michael. *America in the Movies or "Santa Maria, It Had Slipped My Mind."* New York: Basic Books, 1975.

## AMERICAN HISTORY
### Primary Sources

Anderson, Walt, ed. *The Age of Protest*. Pacific Palisades, Calif.: Goodyear Publishing Co., 1969.

Bailey, Thomas A., ed. *The American Spirit: United States History as Seen by Contemporaries*. Boston: D. C. Heath & Co., 1963.

Bell, Daniel. *The End of Ideology: On the Exhaustion of Political Ideas in the Fifties*. Glencoe, Ill.: Free Press, 1960.

————, ed. *The Radical Right: The New American Right Expanded and Updated*. Garden City, N.Y.: Doubleday & Co., 1963.

Boorstin, Daniel. *The Genius of American Politics*. Chicago: University of Chicago Press, 1953.

Buckley, William F., Jr. *Up from Liberalism.* New York: Bantam Books, 1968.

Eisinger, Chester E., ed. *The 1940s: Profile of a Nation in Crisis.* Garden City, N.Y.: Anchor Books, 1969.

Fine, Benjamin. *1,000,000 Delinquents.* Cleveland: World Publishing Co., 1955.

Fromm, Erich. *Escape from Freedom.* New York: Holt, Rinehart, & Winston, 1941.

————. *The Sane Society.* New York: Rinehart & Co., 1955.

Goldwater, Barry. *The Conscience of a Conservative.* New York: Hillman Books, 1960.

Goodman, Paul. *Growing Up Absurd.* New York: Vintage Books, 1960.

Grob, Gerald N., and Beck, Robert N. *Ideas in America: Source Readings in the Intellectual History of the United States.* New York: Free Press, 1970.

Harrington, Michael. *The Other America: Poverty in the United States.* Baltimore: Penguin Books, 1973.

Hoffman, Abbie [Free]. *Revolution for the Hell of It.* New York: Pocket Books, 1970.

Kennedy, John F. *Profiles in Courage.* New York: Pocket Books, 1957.

Kessler, Henry H. *Rehabilitation of the Physically Handicapped.* New York: Columbia University Press, 1953.

Kirk, Russell. *The Conservative Mind: From Burke to Santayana.* Chicago: Henry Regnery Co., 1953.

Kluckhohn, Clyde. "Have There Been Discernible Shifts in American Values during the Past Generation?" *The American Style.* Edited by Elting Morison. New York: Harper & Brothers, 1958.

Lippmann, Walter. *The Public Philosophy.* New York: Mentor Books, 1955.

MacDonald, Dwight. *Against the American Grain.* New York: New York University Press, 1971.

Marcuse, Herbert. *One-Dimensional Man: Studies in the Ideology of Advanced Industrial Society.* Boston: Beacon Press, 1966.

Mead, Margaret. *And Keep Your Powder Dry: An Anthropologist Looks at America.* New York: William Morrow & Co., 1943.

Mills, C. Wright. *The Power Elite.* New York: Oxford University Press, 1956.

————. *White Collar: The American Middle Class.* New York: Oxford University Press, 1953.

200     SHOWDOWN

Niebuhr, Reinhold. *The Children of Light and the Children of Darkness: A Vindication of Democracy and a Critique of Its Traditional Defense.* New York: Charles Scribner's Sons, 1944.

Packard, Vance. *The Hidden Persuaders.* New York: David McKay Co., 1957.

————. *The Status Seekers: An Exploration of Class Behavior in America and the Hidden Barriers That Affect You, Your Community, Your Future.* New York: David McKay Co., 1959.

Reich, Charles A. *The Greening of America.* New York: Bantam Books, 1971.

Riesman, David; Denney, Reuel; and Glazer, Nathan. *The Lonely Crowd.* New Haven, Conn.: Yale University Press, 1950.

Rosenberg, Bernard, ed. *Analyses of Contemporary Society.* New York: Thomas Y. Crowell Co., 1966.

Rossiter, Clinton. *Conservatism in America: The Thankless Persuasion.* New York: Alfred A. Knopf, 1955.

Roszak, Theoder. *The Making of a Counter Culture: Reflections on the Technocratic Society and Its Youthful Opposition.* Garden City, N.Y., Anchor Books, 1969.

Satin, Joseph, ed. *The 1950s: America's Placid Decade.* Boston: Houghton Mifflin Co., 1960.

Schlesinger, Arthur M., Jr. *The Vital Center: The Politics of Freedom.* Boston: Houghton Mifflin Co., 1949.

Spock, Benjamin. *The Common Sense Book of Baby and Child Care.* New York: Duell, Sloan & Pearce, 1957.

U.S., Congress. Senate. Committee on the Judiciary. *Juvenile Delinquency: Comic Books, Motion Pictures, Obscene and Pornographic Materials, Television Programs.* New York: Greenwood Press, 1969.

Whyte, William H., Jr. *The Organization Man.* Garden City, N.Y.: Doubleday Anchor Books, 1956.

### Secondary Sources

Baker, Donald G., and Sheldon, Charles H. *Postwar America: The Search for Identity.* Beverly Hills, Calif.: Glencoe Press, 1969.

Berman, Ronald. *America in the Sixties: An Intellectual History.* New York: Free Press, 1968.

Brooks, John. *The Great Leap: The Past Twenty-Five Years in America.* New York: Harper Colophon Books, 1968.

Christie, Jean, and Dinnerstein, Leonard, eds. *America since World*

*War II: Historical Interpretations.* New York: Praeger Publishers, 1976.

Curti, Merle. *The Growth of American Thought.* 3d ed. New York: Harper & Row, 1964.

Degler, Carl. *Affluence and Anxiety, 1945–Present.* Glenview, Ill.: Scott, Foresman & Co., 1968.

Franklin, John Hope. *From Slavery to Freedom: A History of Negro Americans.* New York: Vintage Books, 1969.

Goldman, Eric F. *The Crucial Decade—And After: America 1945–1960.* New York: Vintage Books, 1960.

Grantham, Dewey W. *The United States since 1945: The Ordeal of Power.* New York: McGraw-Hill, 1976.

Hamby, Alonzo. *The Imperial Years: The United States since 1939.* Weybright & Talley, 1976.

Hartshorne, Thomas L. *The Distorted Image: Changing Conceptions of the American Character since Turner.* Cleveland: Press of Case Western Reserve University, 1968.

Heath, Jim F. *Decade of Disillusionment: The Kennedy-Johnson Years.* Bloomington: Indiana University Press, 1975.

Higham, John. *Writing American History.* Bloomington: Indiana University Press, 1970.

Hodgson, Godfrey. *America in Our Time.* Garden City, N.J.: Doubleday & Co., 1976.

Jordan, Winthrop D. *White over Black: American Attitudes toward the Negro, 1500–1812.* Baltimore: Penguin Books, 1969.

Josephson, Eric, and Josephson, Mary, eds. *Man Alone: Alienation in Modern Society.* New York: Dell Publishing Co., 1962.

Kendrick, Alexander. *The Wound Within: America in the Vietnam Years, 1945–1974.*

Koppes, Clayton R., and Black, Gregory D. "What to Show the World: The Office of War Information and Hollywood, 1942–1945." *Journal of American History* 64 (June 1977):87–105.

Leuchtenburg, William E. *A Troubled Feast: American Society since 1945.* Boston: Little Brown & Co., 1973.

Marcus, Robert D., and Burner, David, eds. *America since 1945.* New York: St. Martin's Press, 1977.

———. *A Brief History of the United States since 1945.* New York: St. Martin's Press, 1975.

Miller, Douglas T., and Nowak, Marion. *The Fifties: The Way We Really Were.* Garden City, N.Y., Doubleday & Co., 1977.

Nash, Roderick. *The Nervous Generation: American Thought, 1917–1930*. Chicago: Rand McNally & Co., 1971.

Olson, Keith. *The G.I. Bill, the Veterans, and the Colleges*. Lexington: University Press of Kentucky, 1974.

O'Neill, William. *Coming Apart: An Informal History of America in the 1960s*. Chicago: Quadrangle Books, 1971.

Pells, Richard H. *Radical Visions and American Dreams: Culture and Social Thought in the Depression Years*. New York: Harper & Row, 1973.

Rosenburg, Norman L.; Rosenburg, Emily; and Moore, James R. *In Our Times: America since World War II*. Englewood Cliffs, N.J.: Prentice-Hall, 1976.

Schaar, John H. *Escape from Authority: The Perspectives of Erich Fromm*. New York: Harper Torchbooks, 1961.

Slotkin, Richard. *Regeneration through Violence: The Mythology of the American Frontier, 1600–1860*. Middletown, Conn.: Wesleyan University Press, 1973.

Weber, Ronald, ed. *America in Change: Reflections on the '60s and '70s*. Notre Dame, Ind.: University of Notre Dame Press, 1972.

Welter, Rush. "The History of Ideas in America: An Essay in Redefinition." *Journal of American History* 51 (March 1965):599–614.

Wittner, Lawrence S. *Cold War America: From Hiroshima to Watergate*. New York: Praeger Publishers, 1974.

Zinn, Howard. *Postwar America, 1945–1971*. Indianapolis: Bobbs-Merrill Co., 1973.

# FILM TITLE INDEX